John Ruskin, William Dwight Porter Bliss

The communism of John Ruskin

John Ruskin, William Dwight Porter Bliss

The communism of John Ruskin

ISBN/EAN: 9783337273941

Printed in Europe, USA, Canada, Australia, Japan

Cover: Foto ©Suzi / pixelio.de

More available books at **www.hansebooks.com**

THE COMMUNISM

OF

JOHN RUSKIN

OR

"UNTO THIS LAST"; TWO LECTURES FROM
"THE CROWN OF WILD OLIVE";
AND SELECTIONS FROM
"FORS CLAVIGERA."

EDITED BY

W. D. P. BLISS.

"For indeed I am myself a Communist of the old school—reddest also of the red."—"FORS CLAVIGERA."

NEW YORK

THE HUMBOLDT PUBLISHING CO.

CLINTON HALL, ASTOR PLACE.

CONTENTS.

	PAGE
INTRODUCTION BY THE EDITOR,	vii

BOOK I.—UNTO THIS LAST,   1
   PREFACE,   3
   ESSAY I.—THE ROOTS OF HONOR,   11
      II.—THE VEINS OF WEALTH,   31
      III.—QUI JUDICATIS TERRAM,   46
      IV.—AD VALOREM,   66

BOOK II.—TWO LECTURES FROM THE CROWN OF WILD OLIVE,   103
   PREFACE,   105
   LECTURE I.—WORK,   119
      II—TRAFFIC,   151

BOOK III.—SELECTIONS FROM FORS CLAVIGERA,   177
   PREFACE BY THE EDITOR,   179
   I.—COMMUNISM,   183
   II.—FREEDOM AND SLAVERY,   188
   III.—MACHINERY,   189
   IV.—TAXES,   191
   V.—CLERGYMEN,   195
   VI.—CARLYLE,   197
   VII.—EXPECTANTS OF TURNIPS,   198
   VIII.—RICH?   199
   IX.—INTEREST,   201
   X.—ST. GEORGE'S COMPANY,   213
   XI.—THE END OF THE WHOLE MATTER,   225

INTRODUCTION.

DO you read Ruskin's *Fors Clavigera?*" Carlyle asked of Emerson, "there is nothing going on among us so notable to me." "I venerate him as one of the greatest teachers of the age; . . . he teaches with the inspiration of a Hebrew Prophet"—such was George Eliot's estimate of Ruskin. Surely Ruskin needs no introduction to the world. The verdict of these two grand-jurymen in the court of letters is borne out by the testimony of witnesses from every portion of the globe. But of Ruskin's social teaching, of his message to society, of his gospel of the life in common,—of this we would say a word—not that *he* needs this either, but that *we* need it, —we need it to rightly appreciate and take home his message to our hearts.

The production of a true social form has been the supreme task given to the nineteenth century. What is Ruskin's place; what his message; what his contribution to the century?

Ruskin is first and foremost a Teacher. He has not originated. He is not the originator of a new system, of a new order, even of a new philosophy. He says somewhere of himself: "I have never applied myself to discover anything, being content to praise what had already been discovered, so that no true disciple of mine will ever be a Ruskinian." He will be something better, his disciples add; he will be one of God's men, with truer, deeper, joy, seeing higher, diviner beauty in the world because Ruskin has shown it to him. Ruskin's Gospel, says one of those whom Ruskin has clung to, is a gospel not of a "news" but "like that of Jesus, a gospel of glad tidings."

And let us not think it a disparagement to Ruskin that he was not an originator. Was Jesus Christ an originator? Did Christ establish a new order? Was Christianity aught but the simple flowering of old Jewish faith? Did Christ come to destroy or to fulfill? Fulfillment is the higher task. Many a man can see a truth, who cannot live it. Jesus Christ lived the truth. His new commandment was more literally a new *command*, the reissuing of old orders. Before Christ came men knew that they should love one another. The secret of Jesus was that he led men in the loving of their neighbors. Is not this the secret too of John Ruskin, not so much that he created Beauty, but that he leads men to love it, helps them to live it—true life, the beauty of Truth, the grace of Sincerity, the Gospel of Noble Things? In this high function of the Teacher, Ruskin, in his line, stands unapproached.

But *how* does he do this? "There are diversities of gifts, but the same spirit. . . . . To one is given by the spirit the word of wisdom; to another the word of knowledge by the same spirit; to another faith by the same spirit; to another the working of miracles; to another prophecy; to another discerning of spirits; to another divers kinds of tongues; to another the interpretation of tongues:" is not this last best gift, Ruskin's gift? could any man ever interpret as does John Ruskin? And is it not the best gift? Can anything be better than to take the truth of God and bring it home to the hearts and lives of men? Was not this His gift who was "The Word" made manifest?

Here is Ruskin's power, Interpretation. Whether it be a Vision of St. Ursula, by Carpaccio, "A Bible of Amiens," or a bit of lapis-lazuli from "St. Mark's Rest," who can ever read it and find in it anything that John Ruskin has not found? Who after Ruskin's reading of it, can ever read it differently?

And yet Ruskin is a true teacher. He teaches *you* to read. He refuses to be systematic. He reads a word here, a line there, but he bids you to do your own reading. He simply shows you how. This is Ruskin's gift, in all his writing.

Now how does he apply this to Social Problems?

Is he not here too a teacher,—a teacher, not an originator,—and as a teacher, above all else an interpreter? He certainly is not an originator in Social Ethics. There is no social gospel according to Ruskin, in the sense of a

Gospel according to Jean Jacques Rousseau. Ruskin is no Robert Owen, no Fourier, no Henry George, no Edward Bellamy. He is even different from William Morris; he has created no Utopia. God's world is good enough for John Ruskin. His is the diviner task of interpreting God's laws for the world that is. He has chosen that better part of sitting at the feet of Truth and showing what it is to be true in social life, and that part shall not be taken from him.

This means no disparagement to Utopia dreamers. They have their place. Do not *you* dare to despise them: child of the present, satisfied with the present, you who are doing nothing, *not even dreaming*, lying drunken with selfishness; when you wake, only waking to speak frothy words of idle gossip. Utopias have their place, only it is not the highest place. As Mrs. Besant tells us: "There are two ways in which the scheme for future organization of industry may be constructed. Of these, by far the easier and less useful is the sketching of Utopia, an intellectual gymnastic in which a power of coherent and vivid imagination is the one desideratum . . . . . The second way is less attractive, less easy, but more useful. Starting from the present state of society, it seeks to discover the tendencies underlying it, to trace those tendencies to their natural out-working in institutions."

This was Ruskin's way. He reads not dreams; he reads the eternal in the present.

But see how he reads—how differently from Carlyle. Both are seers; both read the eternal in the present; both find God everywhere. But Carlyle sees things as they are; Ruskin sees things as they are *and as they ought to be.* Carlyle dwells in the eternal verities; Ruskin shows how to transform negations into verities. Carlyle drives the plowshare of exposure through the hard crusts of society and social order. Into the yawning furrows, Ruskin drops the quickening seeds of truth. Where Carlyle is destructive, Ruskin is constructive; Carlyle burns to free man from the yoke of circumstance; Ruskin leads man to truer life in serving the beautiful and true; Carlyle dwells amid the smoke and thunders of Sinai's law; Ruskin bids us live and love as children of the Father, full of grace and truth.

Such is Ruskin's place in the development of the Social form, a teacher, teaching not by law, but by suggestion, by quickening, by fertilizing, by example, not with system, but with lightning flash, radiating upon mind far vistas of the truth. To-day among the Socialists of the world not many will be found who in the views they now hold call Ruskin Master, but many and many a thoughtful one will tell you that they were led to Socialism by John Ruskin.

Second, his teaching. What does Ruskin teach? What is his Gospel? Like every true Gospel, it is a simple one and yet capable of infinite expansion, and of glorious statement. The essence of his social teaching may perhaps be put in a single phrase, one of his own phrases: "There is no wealth but life, life including all its powers of love, of joy, and of admiration."

From this simple teaching spring as from a corner stone all the noble pillars and portions of his structure. Because noble life is wealth, it follows with Ruskin, that that country is the richest which nourishes the greatest number of noble and happy human beings; that that man is wealthiest, who, having perfected the functions of his own life to the utmost, has also the widest helpful influence, both personal, and by means of his possessions, over the lives of others.

Moreover because life is wealth, it follows that only that which contributes life has a right to return in wealth, hence that *interest*, the return of money for the use of dead money is wrong,—that only those have a right to share in the products of industry who have put into the operation some industry themselves, some outgo of their own life.

These two conceptions, the law of wealth and the law of service, run through all of Ruskin's works, and from them what mighty truths he teaches! The one thought flashes out for example such a crystal phrase as that where he defines wealth as "the possession of the valuable by the valiant;" the other gives us his exhortation to Englishmen and English women to become workers—"Soldiers of the Plowshare as well as Soldiers of the Sword."

It will be at once seen whither such principles must lead.

Ruskin taught from them, *first*, the great law of "Property to whom proper"—or that land and tools belong to those who can use them; *Secondly*, that he who can should use his tools—use his tools to develop life, the highest life in himself and in others; *Thirdly*, that this highest life can only be by coöperation instead of competition, the thought of what we can give rather than of what we can get, the thought of what we are rather than of what we have. This added to Ruskin's teaching as regards art constitutes Ruskin's social system. His theory of art and his theory of society he never divorces because they were both part of his one theory of life. Of art he taught—he himself tells us—first, that the life of art is in religion; secondly, that its food is in the ocular and passionate love of nature; thirdly, that its health is in the humility of the artists. Applying this to his social teaching, his outcome was that Society should be a coöperation or communism of artists, submitting themselves humbly to the law of love, and in the joy of beauty working to produce the highest and the noblest that is in them.

How near this is to Socialism is at once apparent—to Socialism, we say, not Communism or Nationalism.

Ruskin, it is true, calls himself a Communist—in his own strong phrase, "the reddest of the red;" but we believe that he was really much nearer to Socialism. In equality of property he did not believe. In creating his St. George's Guild he distinctly says that there should be "no equality upon it, but recognition of every betterness and reprobation of every worseness." This certainly is opposed to both Communism and Nationalism, but it is in exact accord with the great Socialist and Christian principle of "every man according to his work." In almost all things Ruskin is in accord with Socialism. He believes in government, in the State; he believes in the coöperation of workers in the State; he believes in award for worth; he does not believe in interest; he does not believe in the capitalist; he is the bitterest foe of the Wage System and of the *Laissez faire* political economy.

Ruskin is not, however, a Socialist in all things. He is politically (in his writings) a Conservative, not a Radical. His Socialism is in form paternal, not fraternal. He would not seek for reform through political action. In all this he appears to be the very opposite of a Socialist. Socialism is essentially fraternal, not paternal. It is radical, not conservative; it believes in political action; it is democratic both in politics and in trade. Ruskin fails in this in part because of his education and environment, but even more because of his artistic temperament, which shrinks from the rough-and-tumble and often prosaic machinery of political life. The Gospel of Art has rarely been married to the Gospel of the Ballot Box. Hence politically Ruskin becomes reactionary, yet he is not truly reactionary. His teachings are so radical, so incisive, so inspired with the true spirit of the noblest Socialism, that it must lead and already has led many of his disciples to strive for Socialism in the very political fields against which Ruskin spoke. In his exaltation of work, in his teaching that work is holy, that work for money is not true work, that every man should be an artist and work in coöperation for the good of all, Ruskin teaches such essential Socialism as to condone all failure to see the necessity of political activity.

Thirdly. His achievement. Ruskin is a successful teacher. His work has been to lead. Those misunderstand life who say that he has failed, because he has not developed a concrete community living according to his ideas. He has in truth been vastly more successful than if he had attempted to do this. He has breathed his spirit into men of all classes everywhere. Yet Ruskin attempted the concrete, although this not so much for the value of the concrete itself, as because, in trying to carry out his ideas, he could alone be consistent and, therefore, be a true teacher to the world. His St. George's Guild was an inevitable consequence of his teaching. "No great arts are practicable," he had taught, "by any people unless they are living contented lives, in pure air, out of the way of unsightly objects and emancipated from unnecessary mechanical occupations. It is simply one part of the practical work I have to do in art teaching, to bring, somewhere, such conditions into existence and to show the working of them." He saw too that teaching by example was the best teaching. "The more I see of writing," he says, "the less I care for it; one may do more with a man by getting ten words spoken to him face to face than by the black-lettering of a whole life's thought." This from the writer of *The Stones of Venice* is testimony indeed. No wonder he strove to carry out his ideas. It is in this light and this light only that his industrial experiments must be viewed, simply as object lessons of his teaching. For this purpose, even at Oxford, he took the little company of students who would follow him and went out pick in hand to try and dig a road. What matter that the result was, according to his own half humorous confession, "about the worst road in the three kingdoms;" that was not the real result; the real result was in teaching the nobility of manual labor, and that "food can only be got out of the ground, and enjoyment out of honesty."

Ruskin's great experiment, however, was his St. George's Guild. There is no need here of lengthy description. In our selections from *Fors Clavigera* we have placed some of Ruskin's own statements of the objects and principles of the Guild. We give here but a few quotations from the valuable account of the Guild, found in Edward Cook's *Studies in Ruskin*. "It was in May, 1871," says Mr. Cook, "that the scheme was first made public. In the *Fors* for that month Mr. Ruskin called on any landlords to come and help him who would like better to be served by men than by iron devils, and any tenants and any workmen who could vow to work and live faithfully for the sake of the joy of their home. All who joined St. George's standard were to do as Mr. Ruskin undertook to do, to give the tenth of what they had and what they earned, not to emigrate with, but to stay in England with and make a happy England of her once more."

The Guild had an agricultural, an industrial and an artistic character. On land bought by the Guild, to which Ruskin himself largely contributed, an attempt was made to carry on an agricultural community according to Ruskin's "Laws of Life." Mr. Cook says of this:

"The agricultural experiments of the St. George's Guild have not been a brilliant success. Perhaps they have not been given a fair chance. Perhaps the times and seasons have been unpropitious. But whatever explanations or excuses there may be, the fact remains that the St. George's farms have produced very little except a plentiful crop of disappointments. Mr. Ruskin has drawn many charming pictures of his ideal settlements; but the realities have for the most part been either grim or grotesque, or (more often) both. The Guild is, however, the owner of several acres of land in different parts of the country, and there is some reason to hope that past failures will lead to future successes. If there are any disciples of Count Tolstoi who, having decided 'what to do,' are casting about for plots of ground on which to do it, they should communicate with the Trustees of St. George's Guild."

The industrial experiments of Mr. Ruskin have been in the way of fostering village industries. Wrote Mr. Ruskin: "Whatever may be the destiny of London, or Paris, or Rome in the future, I have always taught that the problem of right organization of country life was wholly independent of them."

Mr. Ruskin's aim was not to organize industrial villages, but to revive, in existing villages, village industry.

Foremost in work in this direction stands Mr. Albert Flemming's attempt, under Ruskin's influence, to bring back the old industry of the spinning wheel to the homes and villages in Westmoreland. In a measure it has succeeded, as one can see by reading Mr. Flemming's own account of it, printed in *Studies in Ruskin*.

Another experiment was the making of "St. George's cloth" in the Isle of Man, undertaken with Ruskin's help, by Mr. Egbert Rydings. A mill was built in romantic architecture by the St. George's Guild, the motive power being of course, in a Ruskinian mill, water and not steam. This too still exists, though it has passed into other hands than those of the Guild.

The main concrete result of the St. George's Guild, has, however, not unnaturally, been artistic, in the creation and maintenance of the unique and beautiful Ruskin Museum at Meresbrook Hall, Sheffield. Of this, the other day, a friend, once himself a devout Ruskinian and a member of St. George's Company, said to us, "The only outcome of Ruskin's Guild is a Peep Show." It was a shallow judgment. Undoubtedly Mr. Ruskin's teachings are of infinitely greater value than the Museum, but would the teachings be complete without their illustration in this characteristic shrine?

So much of John Ruskin. Of this little collection of a small portion of his teachings we need say but little. In the limited space at our disposal we have placed first, *Unto This Last*, as the best presentation, in brief space, of Ruskin's Political Economy, and as that, of all his writings which he himself calls "best," that is, the truest and most serviceable. Secondly, we have placed two wonderful essays on Work and on Traffic, from *The Crown of Wild Olive*, as essays most needed to-day. Lastly, we have added what selections we could from *Fors Clavigera*, as containing some of Ruskin's noblest and most characteristic utterances on social themes. To these last we have prefixed a special preface. To the other books Ruskin himself has already furnished his readers with a preface.

W. D. P. BLISS.

Linden, May, 1891.

BOOK I.
"UNTO THIS LAST."

FOUR ESSAYS ON THE FIRST PRINCIPLES OF
POLITICAL ECONOMY.

PREFACE

THE four following essays were published eighteen months ago in the *Cornhill Magazine*, and were reprobated in a violent manner, as far as I could hear, by most of the readers they met with.

Not a whit the less, I believe them to be the best, that is to say, the truest, rightest-worded, and most serviceable things I have ever written; and the last of them, having had especial pains spent on it, is probably the best I shall ever write.

"This," the reader may reply, "it might be, yet not therefore well written." Which, in no mock humility, admitting, I yet rest satisfied with the work, though with nothing else that I have done; and purposing shortly to follow out the subjects opened in these papers, as I may find leisure, I wish the introductory statements to be within the reach of any one who may care to refer to them. So I republish the essays as they appeared. One word only is changed, correcting the estimate of a weight; and no word is added.

Although, however, I find nothing to modify in these papers, it is matter of regret to me that the most startling of all the statements in them,—that respecting the necessity of the organization of labor, with fixed wages,—should have found its way into the first essay; it being quite one of the least important, though by no means the least certain, of the positions to be defended. The real gist of these papers, their central meaning and aim, is to give, as I believe for the first time in plain English,—it has often been incidentally given in good Greek by Plato and Xenophon, and good Latin by Cicero and Horace,—a logical definition of WEALTH: such definition being absolutely needed for a basis of economical science. The most reputed essay on that subject which has appeared in modern times, after opening with the statement that "writers on political economy profess to teach, or to investigate,* the nature of wealth," thus follows up the declaration of its thesis— "Every one has a notion,.sufficiently correct for common purposes, of what is meant by wealth. . . . It is no part of the design of this treatise to aim. at metaphysical nicety of definition.†"

Metaphysical nicety, we assuredly do not need; but physical nicety, and logical accuracy, with respect to a physical subject, we as assuredly do.

Suppose the subject of inquiry, instead of being House law (*Oikonomia*), had been Star-law (*Astronomia*), and that, ignoring distinction between stars fixed and wandering, as here between wealth radiant and wealth reflective, the writer had begun thus: "Every one has a notion, sufficiently correct for common purposes, of what is meant by stars. Metaphysical nicety in the definition of a star is not the object of this treatise;"—the essay so opened might yet have been far more true in its final statements, and a thousand-fold more serviceable to the navigator, than any treatise on wealth, which founds its conclusions on the

---

*Which? for where investigation is necessary, teaching is impossible.

† *Principles of Political Economy.* By J. S. Mill. Preliminary remarks, p. 2.

popular conception of wealth, can ever become to the economist.

It was, therefore, the first object of these following papers to give an accurate and stable definition of wealth. Their second object was to show that the acquisition of wealth was finally possible only under certain moral conditions of society, of which quite the first was a belief in the existence and even, for practical purposes, in the attainability of honesty.

Without venturing to pronounce—since on such a matter human judgment is by no means conclusive—what is, or is not, the noblest of God's works, we may yet admit so much of Pope's assertion as that an honest man is among His best works presently visible, and, as things stand, a somewhat rare one; but not an incredible or miraculous work; still less an abnormal one. Honesty is not a disturbing force, which deranges the orbits of economy; but a consistent and commanding force, by obedience to which—and by no other obedience—those orbits can continue clear of chaos.

It is true, I have sometimes heard Pope condemned for the lowness instead of the hight, of his standard:— "Honesty is indeed a respectable virtue; but how much higher may men attain! Shall nothing more be asked of us than that we be honest?"

For the present, good friends, nothing. It seems that in our aspirations to be more than that, we have to some extent lost sight of the propriety of being so much as that. What else we may have lost faith in, there shall be here no question; but assuredly we have lost faith in common honesty, and in the working power of it. And this faith, with the facts on which it may rest, it is quite our first business to recover and keep : not only believing, but even by experience assuring ourselves, that there are yet in the world men who can be restrained from fraud otherwise than by the fear of losing employment;* nay, that it is even accurately in proportion to the number of such men in any State, that the said State does or can prolong its existence.

To these two points, then, the following essays are mainly directed. The subject of the organization of labor is only casually touched upon ; because, if we once can get a sufficient quantity of honesty in our captains, the organization of labor is easy, and will develop itself without quarrel or difficulty ; but if we cannot get honesty in our captains, the organization of labor is for evermore impossible.

The several conditions of its possibility I purpose to examine at length in the sequel. Yet, lest the reader should be alarmed by the hints thrown out during the following investigation of first principles, as if they were leading him into unexpectedly dangerous ground, I will, for his better assurance, state at once the worst of the political creed at which I wish him to arrive.

1. First,—that there should be training schools for youth established, at Government cost,† and under Government discipline, over the whole country ; that every child

---

* "The effectual discipline which is exercised over a workman is not that of his corporation, but of his customers. It is the fear of losing their employment which restrains his frauds, and corrects his negligence." (*Wealth of Nations*, Book I., chap. 10.)

† It will probably be inquired by near-sighted persons, out of what funds such schools could be supported. The expedient modes of direct provision for them I will examine hereafter ; indirectly, they would be far more than self-supporting. The economy in crime alone, (quite one of the most costly articles of luxury in the modern European market,) which such schools would induce, would suffice to support them ten times over. Their economy of labor would be pure gain, and that too large to be presently calculable.

PREFACE. 7

born in the country should, at the parent's wish, be permitted (and, in certain cases, be under penalty required) to pass through them ; and that, in these schools, the child should (with other minor pieces of knowledge hereafter to be considered) imperatively be taught, with the best skill of teaching that the country could produce, the following three things :—

(*a*) the laws of health, and the exercises enjoined by them ;

(*b*) habits of gentleness and justice ; and

(*c*) the calling by which he is to live.

2. Secondly,—that, in connection with these training schools, there should be established, also entirely under Government regulation, manufactories and workshops, for the production and sale of every necessary of life, and for the exercise of every useful art. And that, interfering no whit with private enterprise, nor setting any restraints or tax on private trade, but leaving both to do their best, and beat the Government if they could,—there should, at these Government manufactories and shops, be authoritatively good and exemplary work done, and pure and true substance sold; so that a man could be sure, if he chose to pay the Government price, that he got for his money bread that was bread, ale that was ale, and work that was work.

3. Thirdly,—that any man, or woman, or boy, or girl, out of employment, should be at once received at the nearest Government school, and set to such work as it appeared, on trial, they were fit for, at a fixed rate of wages determinable every year :—that, being found incapable of work through ignorance, they should be taught, or being found incapable of work through sickness, should be tended ; but that being found objecting to work, they should be set, under compulsion of the strictest nature, to the more painful

and degrading forms of necessary toil, especially to that in mines and other places of danger (such danger being, however, diminished to the utmost by careful regulation and discipline) and the due wages of such work be retained—cost of compulsion first abstracted—to be at the workman's command, so soon as he has come to sounder mind respecting the laws of employment.

4. Lastly,—that for the old and destitute, comfort and home should be provided; which provision, when misfortune had been by the working of such a system sifted from guilt, would be honorable instead of disgraceful to the receiver. For (I repeat this passage out of my *Political Economy of Art*, to which the reader is referred for further detail*) "a laborer serves his country with his spade, just as a man in the middle ranks of life serves it with sword, pen, or lancet. If the service be less, and, therefore, the wages during health less, then the reward when health is broken may be less, but not less honorable; and it ought to be quite as natural and straightforward a matter for a laborer to take his pension from his parish, because he has deserved well of his parish, as for a man in higher rank to take his pension from his country, because he has deserved well of his country."

To which statement, I will only add, for conclusion, respecting the discipline and pay of life and death, that, for both high and low, Livy's last words touching Valerius Publicola, "*de publico est elatus*," † ought not to be a dishonorable close of epitaph.

These things, then, I believe, and am about, as I find

---

* Addenda, p. 102.

† "P. Valerius, omnium consensu princeps belli pacisque artibus, anno post moritur; gloriâ ingenti, copiis familiaribus adeo exiguis, ut funeri sumtus deesset: de publico est elatus. Luxêre matronæ ut Brutum."—Lib. II., c. xvi.

power, to explain and illustrate in their various bearings; following out also what belongs to them of collateral inquiry. Here I state them only in brief, to prevent the reader casting about in alarm for my ultimate meaning; yet requesting him, for the present, to remember, that in a science dealing with so subtle elements as those of human nature, it is only possible to answer for the final truth of principles, not for the direct success of plans: and that in the best of these last, what can be immediately accomplished is always questionable, and what can be finally accomplished, inconceivable.

JOHN RUSKIN.

Denmark Hill, 10*th May*, 1862.

"UNTO THIS LAST."

ESSAY I.

THE ROOTS OF HONOR.

AMONG the delusions which at different periods have possessed themselves of the minds of large masses of the human race, perhaps the most curious—certainly the least creditable—is the modern *soi-disant* science of political economy, based on the idea that an advantageous code of social action may be determined irrespectively of the influence of social affection.

Of course, as in the instances of alchemy, astrology, witchcraft, and other such popular creeds, political economy has a plausible idea at the root of it. "The social affections," says the economist, "are accidental and disturbing elements in human nature; but avarice and the desire of progress are constant elements. Let us eliminate the inconstants, and, considering the human being merely as a covetous machine, examine by what laws of labor, purchase, and sale, the greatest accumulative result in wealth is attainable. Those laws once determined, it will be for each individual afterward to introduce as much of the disturbing affectionate element as he chooses, and to determine for himself the result on the new conditions supposed."

This would be a perfectly logical and successful method of analysis, if the accidentals afterward to be introduced were of the same nature as the powers first examined. Supposing a body in motion to be influenced by constant and inconstant forces, it is usually the simplest way of examining its course to trace it first under the persistent conditions, and afterward introduce the causes of variation. But the disturbing elements in the social problem are not of the same nature as the constant ones; they alter the essence of the creature under examination the moment they are added; they operate, not mathematically, but chemically, introducing conditions which render all our previous knowledge unavailable. We made learned experiments upon pure nitrogen, and have convinced ourselves that it is a very manageable gas: but behold! the thing which we have practically to deal with is its chloride; and this, the moment we touch it on our established principles, sends us and our apparatus through the ceiling.

Observe, I neither impugn nor doubt the conclusions of the science, if its terms are accepted. I am simply uninterested in them, as I should be in those of a science of gymnastics which assumed that men had no skeletons. It might be shown, on that supposition, that it would be advantageous to roll the students up into pellets, flatten them into cakes, or stretch them into cables; and that when these results were effected, the re-insertion of the skeleton would be attended with various inconveniences to their constitution. The reasoning might be admirable, the conclusions true, and the science deficient only in applicability. Modern political economy stands on a precisely similar basis. Assuming, not that the human being has no skeleton, but that it is all skeleton, it founds an ossifiant theory of progress on this negation of a soul; and having shown the utmost that may be made of bones, and constructed a number of interesting geometrical figures with death's-heads and humeri, successfully proves the inconvenience of the reappearance of a soul among these corpuscular structures. I do not deny the truth of this theory: I simply deny its applicability to the present phase of the world.

This inapplicability has been curiously manifested during the embarrassment caused by the late strikes of our workmen. Here occurs one of the simplest cases, in a pertinent and positive form, of the first vital problem which political economy has to deal with (the relation between employer and employed); and at a severe crisis, when lives in multitudes, and wealth in masses, are at stake, the political economists are helpless—practically mute; no demonstrable solution of the difficulty can be given by them, such as may convince or calm the opposing parties. Obstinately the masters take one view of the matter; obstinately the operatives another; and no political science can set them at one.

It would be strange if it could, it being not by "science" of any kind that men were ever intended to be set at one. Disputant after disputant vainly strives to show that the interests of the masters are, or are not, antagonistic to those of the men; none of the pleaders ever seeming to remember that it does not absolutely or always follow that the persons must be antagonistic because their interests are. If there is only a crust of bread in the house, and mother and children are starving, their interests are not the same. If the mother eats it, the children want it; if the children eat it, the mother must go hungry to her work. Yet it does not necessarily follow that there will be "antagonism" between them, that they will fight for the crust, and that the mother, being strongest, will get it, and eat it. Neither, in any other case, whatever the relations of the persons may be, can it be assumed for certain that, because their interests are diverse, they must necessarily regard each other with hostility, and use violence or cunning to obtain the advantage.

Even if this were so, and it were as just as it is convenient to consider men as actuated by no other moral influences than those which affect rats or swine, the logical conditions of the question are still indeterminable. It can never be shown generally either that the interests of master and laborer are alike, or that they are opposed; for, according to circumstances, they may be either. It is, indeed, always the interest of both that the work should be rightly done, and a just price obtained for it; but, in the division of profits, the gain of the one may or may not be the loss of the other. It is not the master's interest to pay wages so low as to leave the men sickly and depressed, nor the workman's interest to be paid high wages if the smallness of the master's profit hinders him from enlarging his business, or conducting it in a safe and liberal way. A stoker ought not to desire high pay if the company is too poor to keep the engine-wheels in repair.

And the varieties of circumstances which influence these reciprocal interests are so endless, that all endeavor to deduce rules of action from balance of expediency is in vain. And it is meant to be in vain. For no human actions ever were intended by the Maker of men to be guided by balances of expediency, but by balances of justice. He has, therefore, rendered all endeavors to determine expediency futile for evermore. No man ever knew, or can know, what will be the ultimate result to himself, or to others, of any given line of conduct. But every man may know, and most of us do know, what is a just and unjust act. And all of us· may know also, that the consequences of justice will be ultimately the best possible, both to others and ourselves, though we can neither say what *is* best, now how it is likely to come to pass.

I have said balances of justice, meaning, in the term justice, to include affection,—such affection as one man *owes* to another. All right relations between master and operative, and all their best interests, ultimately depend on these.

We shall find the best and simplest illustration of the relations of master and operative in the position of domestic servants.

We will suppose that the master of a household desires only to get as much work out of his servants as he can, at the rate of wages he gives. He never allows them to be idle; feeds them as poorly and lodges them as ill as they will endure, and in all things pushes his requirements to the exact point beyond which he cannot go without forcing the servant to leave him. In doing this, there is no violation on his part of what is commonly called "justice." He agrees with the domestic for his whole time and service, and takes them; the limits of hardship in treatment being fixed by the practice of other masters in his neighborhood; that is to say, by the current rate of wages for domestic labor. If the servant can get a better place, he is free to take one, and the master can only tell what is the real market value of his labor, by requiring as much as he will give.

This is the politico-economical view of the case, according to the doctors of that science; who assert that by this procedure the greatest average of work will be obtained from the servant, and, therefore, the greatest benefit to the community, and through the community, by reversion, to the servant himself.

That, however, is not so. It would be so if the servant were an engine of which the motive power was steam, magnetism, gravitation, or any other agent of calculable force. But he being, on the contrary, an engine whose motive power is a Soul, the force of this very peculiar agent, as an unknown quantity, enters into all the political economist's equations, without his knowledge, and falsifies every one of their results. The largest quantity of work will not be done by this curious engine for pay, or under pressure, or by help of any kind of fuel which may be applied by the chaldron. It will be done only when the motive force, that is to say, the will or spirit of the creature, is brought to its greatest strength by its own proper fuel; namely, by the affections.

It may indeed happen, and does happen often, that if the master is a man of sense and energy, a large quantity of material work may be done under mechanical pressure, enforced by strong will and guided by wise method; also it may happen, and does happen often, that if the master is indolent and weak (however good-natured), a very small quantity of work, and that bad, may be produced by the servant's undirected strength, and contemptuous gratitude. But the universal law of the matter is that, assuming any given quantity of energy and sense in master and servant, the greatest material result obtainable by them will be, not through antagonism to each other, but through affection for each other; and that if the master, instead of endeavoring to get as much work as possible from the servant, seeks rather to render his appointed and necessary work beneficial to him, and to forward his interests in all just and wholesome ways, the real amount of work ultimately done, or of good rendered, by the person so cared for, will indeed be the greatest possible.

Observe, I say, "of good rendered," for a servant's work is not necessarily or always the best thing he can give his master. But good of all kinds, whether in material service, in protective watchfulness of his master's interest and credit, or in joyful readiness to seize unexpected and irregular occasions of help.

Nor is this one whit less generally true because indulgence will be frequently abused, and kindness met with ingratitude. For the servant who, gently treated, is ungrateful, treated ungently, will be revengeful; and the man who is dishonest to a liberal master will be injurious to an unjust one.

In any case, and with any person, this unselfish treatment will produce the most effective return. Observe, I am here considering the affections wholly as a motive power; not at all as things in themselves desirable or noble, or in any other way abstractedly good. I look at them simply as an anomalous force, rendering every one of the ordinary political economist's calculations nugatory; while, even if he desired to introduce this new element into his estimates, he has no power of dealing with it; for the affections only become a true motive power when they ignore every other motive and condition of political economy. Treat the servant kindly, with the idea of turning his gratitude to account, and you will get, as you deserve, no gratitude, nor any value for your kindness; but treat him kindly without any economical purpose, and all economical purposes will be answered; in this, as in all other matters, whosoever will save his life shall lose it, and whoso loses it shall find it.*

---

*The difference between the two modes of treatment, and between their effective material results, may be seen very accurately by a comparison of the relations of Esther and Charlie in *Bleak*

The next clearest and simplest example of relation between master and operative is that which exists between the commander of a regiment and his men.

Supposing the officer only desires to apply the rules of discipline so as, with least trouble to himself, to make the regiment most effective, he will not be able, by any rules, or administration of rules, on this selfish principle, to develop the full strength of his subordinates. If a man of sense and firmness, he may, as in the former instance, produce a better result than would be obtained by the irregular kindness of a weak officer; but let the sense and firmness be the same in both cases, and assuredly the officer who has the most direct personal relations with his men, the most care for their interests, and the most value for their lives, will develop their effective strength, through their

---

House, with those of Miss Brass and the Marchioness in *Master Humphrey's Clock*.

The essential value and truth of Dickens's writings have been unwisely lost sight of by many thoughtful persons, merely because he presents his truth with some color of caricature. Unwisely, because Dickens's caricature, though often gross, is never mistaken. Allowing for his manner of telling them, the things he tells us are always true. I wish that he could think it right to limit his brilliant exaggeration to works written only for public amusement; and when he takes up a subject of high national importance, such as that which he handled in *Hard Times*, that he would use severer and more accurate analysis. The usefulness of that work (to my mind, in several respects, the greatest he has written) is with many persons seriously diminished because Mr. Bounderby is a dramatic monster, instead of a characteristic example of a worldly master; and Stephen Blackpool a dramatic perfection, instead of a characteristic example of an honest workman. But let us not lose the use of Dickens's wit and insight, because he chooses to speak in a circle of stage fire. He is entirely right in his main drift and purpose in every book he has written; and all of them, but especially *Hard Times*, should be studied with close and earnest care by persons interested in social questions. They will find much that is partial, and, because partial, apparently unjust; but if they examine all the evidence on the other side, which Dickens seems to overlook, it will appear, after all their trouble, that his view was the finally right one, grossly and sharply told.

affection for his own person, and trust in his character, to a degree wholly unattainable by other means. The law applies still more stringently as the numbers concerned are larger; a charge may often be successful, though the men dislike their officers; a battle has rarely been won, unless they loved their general.

Passing from these simple examples to the more complicated relations existing between a manufacturer and his workmen, we are met first by certain curious difficulties, resulting, apparently, from a harder and colder state of moral elements. It is easy to imagine an enthusiastic affection existing among soldiers for the colonel. Not so easy to imagine an enthusiastic affection among cotton-spinners for the proprietor of the mill. A body of men associated for purposes of robbery (as a Highland clan in ancient times) shall be animated by perfect affection, and every member of it be ready to lay down his life for the life of his chief. But a band of men associated for purposes of legal production and accumulation is usually animated, it appears, by no such emotions, and none of them is in anywise willing to give his life for the life of his chief. Not only are we met by this apparent anomaly, in moral matters, but by others connected with it, in administration of system. For a servant or a soldier is engaged at a definite rate of wages, for a definite period; but a workman at a rate of wages variable according to the demand for labor, and with the risk of being at any time thrown out of his situation by chances of trade. Now, as, under these contingencies, no action of the affections can take place, but only an explosive action of *dis*affections, two points offer themselves for consideration in the matter.

The first—How far the rate of wages may be so regulated as not to vary with the demand for labor.

The second—How far it is possible that bodies of workmen may be engaged and maintained at such fixed rate of wages (whatever the state of trade may be), without enlarging or diminishing their number, so as to give them permanent interest in the establishment with which they are connected, like that of the domestic servants in an old family, or an *esprit de corps*, like that of the soldiers in a crack regiment.

The first question is, I say, how far it may be possible to fix the rate of wages irrespectively of the demand for labor.

Perhaps one of the most curious facts in the history of human error is the denial by the common political economist of the possibility of thus regulating wages; while for all the important, and much of the unimportant, labor on the earth, wages are already so regulated.

We do not sell our prime-ministership by Dutch auction; nor, on the decease of a bishop, whatever may be the general advantages of simony, do we (yet) offer his diocese to the clergyman who will take the episcopacy at the lowest contract. We (with exquisite sagacity of political economy!) do indeed sell commissions, but not openly, generalships: sick, we do not inquire for a physician who takes less than a guinea; litigious, we never think of reducing six-and-eightpence to four-and-sixpence; caught in a shower, we do not canvass the cabmen, to find out who values his driving at less than sixpence a mile.

It is true that in all these cases there is, and in every conceivable case there must be, ultimate reference to the presumed difficulty of the work, or number of candidates for the office. If it were thought that the labor necessary to make a good physician would be gone through by a sufficient number of students with the prospect of only half-guinea fees, public consent would soon withdraw the unnecessary half-guinea. In this ultimate sense, the price of labor is indeed always regulated by the demand for it; but so far as the practical and immediate administration of the matter is regarded, the best labor always has been, and is, as *all* labor ought to be, paid by an invariable standard.

"What!" the reader, perhaps, answers amazedly: "pay good and bad workmen alike?"

Certainly. The difference between one prelate's sermons and his successor's,—or between one physician's opinion and another's,—is far greater, as respects the qualities of mind involved, and far more important in result to you personally, than the difference between good and bad laying of bricks (though that is greater than most people suppose). Yet you pay with equal fee, contentedly, the good and bad workmen upon your soul, and the good and bad workmen upon your body; much more may you pay, contentedly, with equal fees, the good and bad workmen upon your house.

"Nay, but I choose my physician and (?) my clergyman, thus indicating my sense of the quality of their work." By all means, also, choose your bricklayer; that is the proper reward of the good workman, to be "chosen." The natural and right system respecting all labor is, that it should be paid at a fixed rate, but the good workman employed, and the bad workman unemployed. The false, unnatural, and destructive system is when the bad workman is allowed to offer his work at half-price, and either take the place of the good, or force him by his competition to work for an inadequate sum.

This equality of wages, then, being the first object toward which we have to discover the directest available road; the second is, as above stated, that of maintaining constant numbers of workmen in employment, whatever may be the accidental demand for the article they produce.

I believe the sudden and extensive inequalities of demand which necessarily arise in the mercantile operations of an active nation, constitute the only essential difficulty which has to be overcome in a just organization of labor. The subject opens into too many branches to admit of being investigated in a paper of this kind; but the following general facts bearing on it may be noted.

The wages which enable any workman to live are necessarily higher, if his work is liable to intermission, than if it is assured and continuous; and however severe the struggle for work may become, the general law will always hold, that men must get more daily pay if, on the average, they can only calculate on work three days a week, than they would require if they were sure of work six days a week. Supposing that a man cannot live on less than a shilling a day, his seven shillings he must get, either for three days' violent work, or six days' deliberate work. The tendency of all modern mercantile operations is to throw both wages and trade into the form of a lottery, and to make the workman's pay depend on intermittent exertion, and the principal's profit on dexterously used chance.

In what partial degree, I repeat, this may be necessary, in consequence of the activities of modern trade, I do not here investigate; contenting myself with the fact that in its fatalest aspects it is assuredly unnecessary, and results merely from love of gambling on the part of the masters, and from ignorance and sensuality in the men. The masters cannot bear to let any opportunity of gain escape them, and frantically rush at every gap and breach in the walls of Fortune, raging to be rich, and affronting, with impatient covetousness, every risk of ruin; while the men prefer three days of violent labor, and three days of drunkenness, to six days of moderate work and wise rest. There is no way in which a principal, who really desires to help his workmen, may do it more effectually than by checking these disorderly habits both in himself and them; keeping his own business operations on a scale which will enable him to pursue them securely, not yielding to temptations of precarious gain; and, at the same time, leading his workmen into regular habits of labor and life, either by inducing them rather to take low wages in the form of a fixed salary, than high wages, subject to the chance of their being thrown out of work; or, if this be impossible, by discouraging the system of violent exertion for nominally high day wages, and leading the men to take lower pay for more regular labor.

In effecting any radical changes of this kind, doubtless there would be great inconvenience and loss incurred by all the originators of movement. That which can be done with perfect convenience and without loss, is not always the thing that most needs to be done, or which we are most imperatively required to do.

I have already alluded to the difference hitherto existing between regiments of men associated for purposes of violence, and for purposes of manufacture; in that the former appear capable of self-sacrifice—the latter, not; which singular fact is the real reason of the general lowness of estimate in which the profession of commerce is held, as compared with that of arms. Philosophically, it does not, at first sight, appear reasonable (many writers have endeavored to prove it unreasonable) that a peaceable and rational person, whose trade is buying and selling, should be held in less honor than an unpeaceable and often irrational person, whose trade is slaying. Nevertheless, the consent of mankind has always, in spite of the philosophers, given precedence to the soldier.

And this is right.

For the soldier's trade, verily and essentially, is not slaying, but being slain. This, without well knowing its own meaning, the world honors it for. A bravo's trade is slaying; but the world has never respected bravos more than merchants; the reason it honors the soldier is, because he holds his life at the service of the State. Reckless he may be—fond of pleasure or of adventure—all kinds of bye-motives and mean impulses may have determined the choice of his profession, and may affect (to all appearance exclusively) his daily conduct in it; but our estimate of him is based on this ultimate fact—of which we are well assured—that, put him in a fortress breach, with all the pleasures of the world behind him, and only death and his duty in front of him, he will keep his face to the front; and he knows that this choice may be put to him at any moment, and has beforehand taken his part—virtually takes such part continually—does, in reality, die daily.

Not less is the respect we pay to the lawyer and physician, founded ultimately on their self-sacrifice. Whatever the learning or acuteness of a great lawyer, our chief respect for him depends on our belief that, set in a judge's seat, he will strive to judge justly, come of it what may. Could we suppose that he would take bribes, and use his acuteness and legal knowledge to give plausibility to iniquitous decisions, no degree of intellect would win for him our respect. Nothing will win it, short of our tacit conviction, that in all important acts of his life justice is first with him; his own interest, second.

In the case of a physician, the ground of the honor we render him is clearer still. Whatever his science, we should shrink from him in horror if we found him regard his patients merely as subjects to experiment upon; much more, if we found that, receiving bribes from persons interested in their deaths, he was using his best skill to give poison in the mask of medicine.

Finally, the principle holds with utmost clearness as it respects clergymen. No goodness of disposition will excuse want of science in a physician or of shrewdness in an advocate; but a clergyman, even though his power of intellect be small, is respected on the presumed ground of his unselfishness and serviceableness.

Now there can be no question but that the tact, foresight, decision, and other mental powers, required for the successful management of a large mercantile concern, if not such as could be compared with those of a great lawyer, general, or divine, would at least match the general conditions of mind required in the subordinate officers of a ship, or of a regiment, or in the curate of a country parish. If, therefore, all the efficient members of the so-called liberal professions are still, somehow, in public estimate of honor, preferred before the head of a commercial firm, the reason must lie deeper than in the measurement of their several powers of mind.

And the essential reason for such preference will be found to lie in the fact that the merchant is presumed to act always selfishly. His work may be very necessary to the community; but the motive of it is understood to be wholly personal. The merchant's first object in all his dealings must be (the public believe) to get as much for himself, and leave as little to his neighbor (or customer) as possible. Enforcing this upon him, by political statute, as the necessary principle of his action; recommending it to him on all occasions, and themselves reciprocally adopting it; proclaiming vociferously, for law of the universe, that a buyer's function is to cheapen, and a seller's to cheat,— the public, nevertheless, involuntarily condemn the man of commerce for his compliance with their own statement, and stamp him forever as belonging to an inferior grade of human personality.

This they will find, eventually, they must give up doing. They must not cease to condemn selfishness; but they will have to discover a kind of commerce which is not exclusively selfish. Or, rather, they will have to discover that there never was, or can be, any other kind of commerce; that this which they have called commerce was not commerce at all, but cozening; and that a true merchant differs as much from a merchant according to laws of modern political economy, as the hero of the *Excursion* from Autolycus. They will find that commerce is an occupation which gentlemen will every day see more need to engage in, rather than in the businesses of talking to men, or slaying them; that, in true commerce, as in true preaching, or true fighting, it is necessary to admit the idea of occasional voluntary loss;—that sixpences have to be lost, as well as lives, under a sense of duty; that the market may have its martyrdoms as well as the pulpit; and trade its heroisms, as well as war.

May have—in the final issue, must have—and only has not had yet, because men of heroic temper have always been misguided in their youth into other fields, not recognizing what is in our days, perhaps, the most important of all fields; so that, while many a zealous person loses his life in trying to teach the form of a gospel, very few will lose a hundred pounds in showing the practice of one.

The fact is, that people never have had clearly explained to them the true functions of a merchant with respect to other people. I should like the reader to be very clear about this.

Five great intellectual professions, relating to daily necessities of life, have hitherto existed—three exist necessarily, in every civilized nation:

The Soldier's profession is to *defend* it.
The Pastor's, to *teach* it.
The Physician's, to *keep it in health*.
The Lawyer's, to *enforce justice*.
The Merchant's, to *provide* for it.

And the duty of all these men is, on due occasion, to *die* for it.

"On due occasion," namely:—
The Soldier, rather than leave his post in battle.
The Physician, rather than leave his post in plague.
The Pastor, rather than teach Falsehood.
The Lawyer, rather than countenance Injustice.
The Merchant—What is *his* "due occasion" of death?

It is the main question for the merchant, as for all of us. For, truly, the man who does not know when to die, does not know how to live.

Observe, the merchant's function (or manufacturer's, for in the broad sense in which it is here used the word must be understood to include both) is to provide for the nation. It is no more his function to get profit for himself out of that provision than it is a clergyman's function to get his stipend. The stipend is a due and necessary adjunct, but not the object, of his life, if he be a true clergyman, any more than his fee (or *honorarium*) is the object of life to a true physician. Neither is his fee the object of life to a true merchant. All three, if true men, have a work to be done irrespective of fee—to be done even at any cost, or for quite the contrary of fee; the pastor's function being to teach, the physician's to heal, and the merchant's, as I have said, to provide. That is to say, he has to understand to their very root the qualities of the thing he deals in, and the means of obtaining or producing it; and he has to apply all his sagacity and energy to the producing or obtaining it in perfect state, and distributing it at the cheapest possible price where it is most needed.

And because the production or obtaining of any commodity involves necessarily the agency of many lives and hands, the merchant becomes in the course of his business the master and governor of large masses of men in a more direct, though less confessed way, than a military officer or pastor; so that on him falls, in great part, the responsibility for the kind of life they lead: and it becomes his duty, not only to be always considering how to produce what he sells in the purest and cheapest forms, but how to make the various employments involved in the production, or transference of it, most beneficial to the men employed.

And as into these two functions, requiring for their right exercise the highest intelligence, as well as patience, kindness, and tact, the merchant is bound to put all his energy, so for their just discharge he is bound, as soldier or physician is bound, to give up, if need be, his life, in such way as may be demanded of him. Two main points he has in his providing function to maintain: first, his engagements (faithfulness to engagements being the real root of all possibilities in commerce); and, secondly, the perfectness and purity of the thing provided; so that, rather than fail in any engagement, or consent to any deterioration, adulteration, or unjust and exorbitant price of that which he provides, he is bound to meet fearlessly any form of distress, poverty, or labor, which may, through maintenance of these points, come upon him.

Again: in his office as governor of the men employed by him, the merchant or manufacturer is invested with a distinctly paternal authority and responsibility. In most cases, a youth entering a commercial establishment is withdrawn altogether from home influence; his master must become his father, else he has, for practical and constant help, no father at hand: in all cases the master's authority, together with the general tone and atmosphere of his business, and the character of the men with whom the youth is compelled in the course of it to associate, have more immediate and pressing weight than the home influence, and will usually neutralize it either for good or evil; so that the only means which the master has of doing justice to the men employed by him is to ask himself sternly whether he is dealing with such subordinate as he would with his own son, if compelled by circumstances to take such a position.

Supposing the captain of a frigate saw it right, or were by any chance obliged, to place his own son in the position of a common sailor; as he would then treat his son, he is bound always to treat every one of the men under him. So, also, supposing the master of a manufactory saw it right, or were by any chance obliged, to place his own son in the position of an ordinary workman; as he would then treat his son, he is bound always to treat every one of his men. This is the only effective, true, or practical RULE which can be given on this point of political economy.

And as the captain of a ship is bound to be the last man to leave his ship in case of wreck, and to share his last crust with the sailors in case of famine, so the manufacturer, in any commercial crisis or distress, is bound to take the suffering of it with his men, and even to take more of it for himself than he allows his men to feel; as a father would in a famine, shipwreck, or battle, sacrifice himself for his son.

All which sounds very strange; the only real strangeness in the matter being, nevertheless, that it should so sound. For all this is true, and that not partially nor theoretically, but everlastingly and practically: all other doctrine than this respecting matters political being false in premises, absurd in deduction, and impossible in practice, consistently with any progressive state of national life; all the life which we now possess as a nation showing itself in the resolute denial and scorn, by a few strong minds and faithful hearts, of the economic principles taught to our multitudes, which principles, so far as accepted, lead straight to national destruction. Respecting the modes and forms of destruction to which they lead, and, on the other hand, respecting the further practical working of true polity, I hope to reason further in a following paper.

ESSAY II.

THE VEINS OF WEALTH.

THE answer which would be made by any ordinary political economist to the statements contained in the preceding paper, is in few words as follows:—
"It is indeed true that certain advantages of a general nature may be obtained by the development of social affections. But political economists never professed, nor profess, to take advantages of a general nature into consideration. Our science is simply the science of getting rich. So far from being a fallacious or visionary one, it is found by experience to be practically effective. Persons who follow its precepts do actually become rich, and persons who disobey them become poor. Every capitalist of Europe has acquired his fortune by following the known laws of our science, and increases his capital daily by an adherence to them. It is vain to bring forward tricks of logic, against the force of accomplished facts. Every man of business knows by experience how money is made, and how it is lost."

Pardon me. Men of business do indeed know how they themselves made their money, or how, on occasion, they lost it. Playing a long-practiced game, they are familiar with the chances of its cards, and can rightly explain their losses and gains. But they neither know who keeps the bank of the gambling-house, nor what other games may be played with the same cards, nor what other losses and gains, far away among the dark streets, are essentially, though invisibly, dependent on theirs in the lighted rooms. They have learned a few, and only a few, of the laws of mercantile economy; but not one of those of political economy.

Primarily, which is very notable and curious, I observe that men of business rarely know the meaning of the word "rich." At least if they know, they do not in their reasonings allow for the fact, that it is a relative word, implying its opposite "poor" as positively as the word "north" implies its opposite "south." Men nearly always speak and write as if riches were absolute, and it were possible, by following certain scientific precepts, for everybody to be rich. Whereas riches are a power like that of electricity, acting only through inequalities or negations of itself. The force of the guinea you have in your pocket depends wholly on the default of a guinea in your neighbor's pocket. If he did not want it, it would be of no use to you; the degree of power it possesses depends accurately upon the need or desire he has for it,—and the art of making yourself rich, in the ordinary mercantile economist's sense, is therefore equally and necessarily the art of keeping your neighbor poor.

I would not contend in this matter (and rarely in any matter), for the acceptance of terms. But I wish the reader clearly and deeply to understand the difference between the two economies, to which the terms "Political" and "Mercantile" might not unadvisably be attached.

Political economy (the economy of a State, or of citizens) consists simply in the production, preservation, and distribution, at fittest time and place, of useful or pleasurable things. The farmer who cuts his hay at the right time; the shipwright who drives his bolts well home in sound wood; the builder who lays good bricks in well-tempered mortar; the housewife who takes care of her furniture in the parlor, and guards against all waste in her kitchen; and the singer who rightly disciplines, and never overstrains her voice: are all political economists in the true and final sense; adding continually to the riches and well-being of the nation to which they belong.

But mercantile economy, the economy of "merces" or of "pay," signifies the accumulation, in the hands of individuals, of legal or moral claim upon, or power over, the labor of others; every such claim implying precisely as much poverty or debt on one side, as it implies riches or right on the other.

It does not, therefore, necessarily involve an addition to the actual property, or well-being, of the State in which it exists. But since this commercial wealth, or power over labor, is nearly always convertible at once into real property, while real property is not always convertible at once into power over labor, the idea of riches among active men in civilized nations, generally refers to commercial wealth; and in estimating their possessions, they rather calculate the value of their horses and fields by the number of guineas they could get for them, than the value of their guineas by the number of horses and fields they could buy with them.

There is, however, another reason for this habit of mind; namely, that an accumulation of real property is of little use to its owner, unless, together with it, he has commercial power over labor. Thus, suppose any person to be put in possession of a large estate of fruitful land, with rich beds of gold in its gravel, countless herds of cattle in its pastures; houses, and gardens, and storehouses full of useful stores, but suppose, after all, that he could get no servants? In order that he may be able to have servants, some one in his neighborhood must be poor, and in want of his gold—

or his corn. Assume that no one is in want of either, and that no servants are to be had. He must, therefore, bake his own bread, make his own clothes, plow his own ground, and shepherd his own flocks. His gold will be as useful to him as any other yellow pebbles on his estate. His stores must rot, for he cannot consume them. He can eat no more than another man could eat, and wear no more than another man could wear. He must lead a life of severe and common labor to procure even ordinary comforts; he will be ultimately unable to keep either houses in repair, or fields in cultivation; and forced to content himself with a poor man's portion of cottage and garden, in the midst of a desert of waste land, trampled by wild cattle, and encumbered by ruins of palaces, which he will hardly mock at himself by calling "his own."

The most covetous of mankind, would with small exultation, I presume, accept riches of this kind on these terms. What is really desired, under the name of riches, is, essentially, power over men; in its simplest sense, the power of obtaining for our own advantage the labor of servant, tradesman, and artist; in wider sense, authority of directing large masses of the nation to various ends (good, trivial, or hurtful, according to the mind of the rich person). And this power of wealth of course is greater or less in direct proportion to the poverty of the men over whom it is exercised, and in inverse proportion to the number of persons who are as rich as ourselves, and who are ready to give the same price for an article of which the supply is limited. If the musician is poor, he will sing for small pay, as long as there is only one person who can pay him; but if there be two or three, he will sing for the one who offers him most. And thus the power of the riches of the patron (always imperfect and doubtful, as we shall see presently, even when most authoritative) depends first on the poverty of the artist, and then on the limitation of the number of equally wealthy persons, who also want seats at the concert. So that, as above stated, the art of becoming "rich," in the common sense, is not absolutely nor finally the art of accumulating much money for ourselves, but also of contriving that our neighbors shall have less. In accurate terms, it is "the art of establishing the maximum inequality in our own favor."

Now the establishment of such inequality cannot be shown in the abstract to be either advantageous or disadvantageous to the body of the nation. The rash and absurd assumption that such inequalities are necessarily advantageous, lies at the root of most of the popular fallacies on the subject of political economy. For the eternal and inevitable law in this matter is, that the beneficialness of the inequality depends, first, on the methods by which it was accomplished, and, secondly, on the purposes to which it is applied. Inequalities of wealth, unjustly established, have assuredly injured the nation in which they exist during their establishment; and, unjustly directed, injure it yet more during their existence. But inequalities of wealth justly established, benefit the nation in the course of their establishment; and nobly used, aid it yet more by their existence. That is to say, among every active and well-governed people, the various strength of individuals, tested by full exertion and specially applied to various needs, issues in unequal, but harmonious results, receiving reward or authority according to its class and service;* while in

---

*I have been naturally asked several times, with respect to the sentence in the first of these papers, "the bad workmen unemployed," "But what are you to do with your bad unemployed workmen?" Well, it seems to me the question might have occurred to you

the inactive or ill-governed nation, the gradations of decay and the victories of treason work out also their own rugged system of subjection and success; and substitute, for the melodious inequalities of concurrent power, the iniquitous dominances and depressions of guilt and misfortune.

Thus the circulation of wealth in a nation resembles that of the blood in the natural body. There is one quickness of the current which comes of cheerful emotion or wholesome exercise; and another which comes of shame or of fever. There is a flush of the body which is full of warmth and life; and another which will pass into putrefaction.

The analogy will hold, down even to minute particulars. For as diseased local determination of the blood involves depression of the general health of the system, all morbid

---

before. Your housemaid's place is vacant—you give twenty pounds a year—two girls come for it, one neatly dressed, the other dirtily; one with good recommendations, the other with none. You do not, under these circumstances, usually ask the dirty one if she will come for fifteen pounds, or twelve; and, on her consenting, take her instead of the well-recommended one. Still less do you try to beat both down by making them bid against each other, till you can hire both, one at twelve pounds a year, and the other at eight. You simply take the one fittest for the place, and send away the other, not perhaps concerning yourself quite as much as you should with the question which you now impatiently put to me, "What is to become of her?" For all that I advise you to do, is to deal with workmen as with servants: and verily the question is of weight: "Your bad workman, idler, and rogue—what are you to do with him?"

We will consider of this presently: remember that the administration of a complete system of national commerce and industry cannot be explained in full detail within the space of twelve pages. Meantime, consider whether, there being confessedly some difficulty in dealing with rogues and idlers, it may not be advisable to produce as few of them as possible. If you examine into the history of rogues, you will find they are as truly manufactured articles as anything else, and it is just because our present system of political economy gives so large a stimulus to that manufacture that you may know it to be a false one. We had better seek for a system which will develop honest men, than for one which will deal cunningly with vagabonds. Let us reform our schools, and we shall find little reform needed in our prisons.

local action of riches will be found ultimately to involve a weakening of the resources of the body politic.

The mode in which this is produced may be at once understood by examining one or two instances of the development of wealth in the simplest possible circumstances.

Suppose two sailors cast away on an uninhabited coast, and obliged to maintain themselves there by their own labor for a series of years.

If they both kept their health, and worked steadily, and in amity with each other, they might build themselves a convenient house, and in time come to possess a certain quantity of cultivated land, together with various stores laid up for future use. All these things would be real riches or property; and supposing the men both to have worked equally hard, they would each have right to equal share or use of it. Their political economy would consist merely in careful preservation and just division of these possessions. Perhaps, however, after some time one or other might be dissatisfied with the results of their common farming; and they might in consequence agree to divide the land they had brought under the spade into equal shares, so that each might thenceforward work in his own field and live by it. Suppose that after this arrangement had been made, one of them were to fall ill, and be unable to work on his land at a critical time—say of sowing or harvest.

He would naturally ask the other to sow or reap for him.

Then his companion might say, with perfect justice, "I will do this additional work for you; but if I do it, you must promise to do as much for me at another time. I will count how many hours I spend on your ground, and you shall give me a written promise to work for the same number of hours on mine, whenever I need your help, and you are able to give it."

Suppose the disabled man's sickness to continue, and that under various circumstances, for several years, requiring the help of the other, he on each occasion gave a written pledge to work, as soon as he was able, at his companion's orders, for the same number of hours which the other had given up to him. What will the positions of the two men be when the invalid is able to resume work?

Consider as a "Polis," or state, they will be poorer than they would have been otherwise: poorer by the withdrawal of what the sick man's labor would have produced in the interval. His friend may perhaps have toiled with an energy quickened by the enlarged need, but in the end his own land and property must have suffered by the withdrawal of so much of his time and thought from them; and the united property of the two men will be certainly less than it would have been if both had remained in health and activity.

But the relations in which they stand to each other are also widely altered. The sick man has not only pledged his labor for some years, but will probably have exhausted his own share of the accumulated stores, and will be in consequence for some time dependent on the other for food, which he can only "pay" or reward him for by yet more deeply pledging his own labor.

Supposing the written promises to be held entirely valid (among civilized nations their validity is secured by legal measures*), the person who had hitherto worked for both

---

* The disputes which exist respecting the real nature of money arise more from the disputants examining its functions on different sides, than from any real dissent in their opinions. All money, properly so called, is an acknowledgment of debt; but as such, it may either be considered to represent the labor and property of the

might now, if he chose, rest altogether, and pass his time in idleness, not only forcing his companion to redeem all the engagements he had already entered into, but exacting from him pledges for further labor, to an arbitrary amount, for what food he had to advance to him.

There might not, from first to last, be the least illegality (in the ordinary sense of the word) in the arrangement; but if a stranger arrived on the coast at this advanced epoch of their political economy, he would find one man commercially Rich; the other commercially Poor. He would see, perhaps with no small surprise, one passing his days in idleness; the other laboring for both, and living sparely, in the hope of recovering his independence, at some distant period.

This is, of course, an example of one only out of many ways in which inequality of possession may be established between different persons, giving rise to the mercantile forms of Riches and Poverty. In the instance before us, one of the men might from the first have deliberately chosen to be idle, and to put his life in pawn for present ease; or he might have mismanaged his land, and been compelled to have recourse to his neighbor for food and help, pledging his future labor for it. But what I want the reader to note especially is the fact, common to a large number of typical cases of this kind, that the establishment of the mercantile wealth which consists in a claim upon

---

creditor, or the idleness and penury of the debtor. The intricacy of the question has been much increased by the (hitherto necessary) use of marketable commodities, such as gold, silver, salt, shells, &c., to give intrinsic value or security to currency; but the final and best definition of money is that it is a documentary promise ratified and guaranteed by the nation to give or find a certain quantity of labor on demand. A man's labor for a day is a better standard of value than a measure of any produce, because no produce ever maintains a consistent rate of productibility.

labor, signifies a political diminution of the real wealth which consists in substantial possessions.

Take another example, more consistent with the ordinary course of affairs of trade. Suppose that three men, instead of two, formed the little isolated republic, and found themselves obliged to separate in order to farm different pieces of land at some distance from each other along the coast; each estate furnishing a distinct kind of produce, and each more or less in need of the material raised on the other. Suppose that the third man, in order to save the time of all three, undertakes simply to superintend the transference of commodities from one farm to the other; on condition of receiving some sufficiently remunerative share of every parcel of goods conveyed, or of some other parcel received in exchange for it.

If this carrier or messenger always brings to each estate, from the other, what is chiefly wanted, at the right time, the operations of the two farmers will go on prosperously, and the largest possible result in produce, or wealth, will be attained by the little community. But suppose no intercourse between the land owners is possible, except through the traveling agent; and that, after a time, this agent, watching the course of each man's agriculture, keeps back the articles with which he has been entrusted, until there comes a period of extreme necessity for them, on one side or other, and then exacts in exchange for them all that the distressed farmer can spare of other kinds of produce; it is easy to see that by ingeniously watching his opportunities, he might possess himself regularly of the greater part of the superfluous produce of the two estates, and at last, in some year of severest trial or scarcity, purchase both for himself, and maintain the former proprietors thenceforward as his laborers or his servants.

This would be a case of commercial wealth acquired on the exactest principles of modern political economy. But more distinctly even than in the former instance, it is manifest in this that the wealth of the State, or of the three men considered as a society, is collectively less than it would have been had the merchant been content with juster profit. The operations of the two agriculturists have been cramped to the utmost; and the continual limitations of the supply of things they wanted at critical times, together with the failure of courage consequent on the prolongation of a struggle for mere existence, without any sense of permanent gain, must have seriously diminished the effective results of their labor; and the stores finally accumulated in the merchant's hands will not in anywise be of equivalent value to those which, had his dealings been honest, would have filled at once the granaries of the farmers and his own.

The whole question, therefore, respecting not only the advantage, but even the quantity, of national wealth, resolves itself finally into one of abstract justice. It is impossible to conclude, of any given mass of acquired wealth, merely by the fact of its existence, whether it signifies good or evil to the nation in the midst of which it exists. Its real value depends on the moral sign attached to it, just as sternly as that of a mathematical quantity depends on the algebraical sign attached to it. Any given accumulation of commercial wealth may be indicative, on the one hand, of faithful industries, progressive energies, and productive ingenuities; or, on the other, it may be indicative of mortal luxury, merciless tyranny, ruinous chicane. Some treasures are heavy with human tears, as an ill-stored harvest with untimely rain; and some gold is brighter in sunshine than it is in substance.

And these are not, observe, merely moral or pathetic

attributes of riches, which the seeker of riches may, if he chooses, despise; they are literally and sternly, material attributes of riches, depreciating or exalting, incalculably, the monetary signification of the sum in question. One mass of money is the outcome of action which has created,— another, of action which has annihilated,—ten times as much in the gathering of it; such and such strong hands have been paralyzed, as if they had been numbed by nightshade: so many strong men's courage broken, so many productive operations hindered; this and the other false direction given to labor, and lying image of prosperity set up, on Dura plains dug into seven-times-heated furnaces. That which seems to be wealth may in verity be only the gilded index of far-reaching ruin; a wrecker's handful of coin gleaned from the beach to which he has beguiled an argosy; a camp-follower's bundle of rags unwrapped from the breasts of goodly soldiers dead; the purchase-pieces of potter's fields, wherein shall be buried together the citizen and the stranger.

And therefore, the idea that directions can be given for the gaining of wealth, irrespectively of the consideration of its moral sources, or that any general and technical law of purchase and gain can be set down for national practice, is perhaps the most insolently futile of all that ever beguiled men through their vices. So far as I know, there is not in history record of anything so disgraceful to the human intellect as the modern idea that the commercial text, "Buy in the cheapest market and sell in the dearest," represents, or under any circumstances could represent, an available principle of national economy. Buy in the cheapest market?—yes; but what made your market cheap? Charcoal may be cheap among your roof timbers after a fire, and bricks may be cheap in your streets after an earthquake; but fire and earthquake may not, therefore, be national benefits. Sell in the dearest?—yes, truly; but what made your market dear? You sold your bread well to-day; was it to a dying man who gave his last coin for it, and will never need bread more, or to a rich man who to-morrow will buy your farm over your head; or to a soldier on his way to pillage the bank in which you have put your fortune?

None of these things you can know. One thing only you can know, namely, whether this dealing of yours is a just and faithful one, which is all you need concern yourself about respecting it; sure thus to have done your own part in bringing about ultimately in the world a state of things which will not issue in pillage or in death. And thus every question concerning these things merges itself ultimately in the great question of justice, which, the ground being thus far cleared for it, I will enter upon in the next paper, leaving only, in this, three final points for the reader's consideration.

It has been shown that the chief value and virtue of money consists in its having power over human beings; that, without this power, large material possessions are useless, and to any person possessing such power, comparatively unnecessary. But power over human beings is attainable by other means than by money. As I said a few pages back, the money power is always imperfect and doubtful; there are many things which cannot be retained by it. Many joys may be given to men which cannot be bought for gold, and many fidelities found in them which cannot be rewarded with it.

Trite enough,—the reader thinks. Yes: but it is not so trite,—I wish it were,—that in this moral power, quite inscrutable and immeasurable though it be, there is a monetary value just as real as that represented by more ponderous currencies. A man's hand may be full of invisible gold, and the wave of it, or the grasp, shall do more than another's with a shower of bullion. This invisible gold, also, does not necessarily diminish in spending. Political economists will do well some day to take heed of it, though they cannot take measure.

But further. Since the essence of wealth consists in its authority over men, if the apparent or nominal wealth fail in this power, it fails in essence; in fact, ceases to be wealth at all. It does not appear lately in England, that our authority over men is absolute. The servants show some disposition to rush riotously upstairs, under an impression that their wages are not regularly paid. We should augur ill of any gentleman's property to whom this happened every other day in his drawing-room.

So also, the power of our wealth seems limited as respects the comfort of the servants, no less than their quietude. The persons in the kitchen appear to be ill-dressed, squalid, half-starved. One cannot help imagining that the riches of the establishment must be of a very theoretical and documentary character.

Finally. Since the essence of wealth consists in power over men, will it not follow that the nobler and the more in number the persons are over whom it has power, the greater the wealth? Perhaps it may even appear after some consideration, that the persons themselves *are* the wealth—that these pieces of gold with which we are in the habit of guiding them, are, in fact, nothing more than a kind of Byzantine harness or trappings, very glittering and beautiful in barbaric sight, wherewith we bridle the creatures; but that if these same living creatures could be guided without the fretting and jingling of the Byzants in their mouths and ears, they might themselves be more valuable than their bridles. In fact, it may be discovered that the true veins of wealth are purple—and not in Rock, but in Flesh—perhaps even that the final outcome and consummation of all wealth is in the producing as many as possible full-breathed, bright-eyed, and happy-hearted human creatures. Our modern wealth, I think, has rather a tendency the other way;—most political economists appearing to consider multitudes of human creatures not conducive to wealth, or at best conducive to it only by remaining in a dim-eyed and narrow-chested state of being.

Nevertheless, it is open, I repeat, to serious question, which I leave to the reader's pondering, whether, among national manufactures, that of Souls of a good quality may not at last turn out a quite leadingly lucrative one? Nay, in some far away and yet undreamed-of hour, I can even imagine that England may cast all thoughts of possessive wealth back to the barbaric nations among whom they first arose; and that, while the sands of the Indus and adamant of Golconda may yet stiffen the housings of the charger, and flash from the turban of the slave, she, as a Christian mother, may at last attain to the virtues and the treasures of a Heathen one, and be able to lead forth her Sons, saying,—

"These are MY Jewels."

ESSAY III.

QUI JUDICATIS TERRAM.

SOME centuries before the Christian era, a Jew merchant largely engaged in business on the Gold Coast, and reported to have made one of the largest fortunes of his time (held also in repute for much practical sagacity), left among his ledgers some general maxims concerning wealth, which have been preserved, strangely enough, even to our own days. They were held in considerable respect by the most active traders of the middle ages, especially by the Venetians, who even went so far in their admiration as to place a statue of the old Jew on the angle of one of their principal public buildings. Of late years these writings have fallen into disrepute, being opposed in every particular to the spirit of modern commerce. Nevertheless I shall reproduce a passage or two from them here, partly because they may interest the reader by their novelty; and chiefly because they will show him that it is possible for a very practical and acquisitive tradesman to hold, through a not unsuccessful career, that principle of distinction between well-gotten and ill-gotten wealth, which, partially insisted on in my last paper, it must be our work more completely to examine in this.

He says, for instance, in one place: "The getting of treasure by a lying tongue is a vanity tossed to and fro of them that seek death:" adding in another, with the same meaning (he has a curious way of doubling his sayings): "Treasures of wickedness profit nothing; but justice delivers from death." Both these passages are notable for their assertion of death as the only real issue and sum of attainment by any unjust scheme of wealth. If we read, instead of "lying tongue," "lying label, title, pretense, or advertisement," we shall more clearly perceive the bearing of the words on modern business. The seeking of death is a grand expression of the true course of men's toil in such business. We usually speak as if death pursued us, and we fled from him; but that is only so in rare instances. Ordinarily, he masks himself—makes himself beautiful—all-glorious; not like the King's daughter, all-glorious within, but outwardly: his clothing of wrought gold. We pursue him frantically all our days, he flying or hiding from us. Our crowning success at threescore and ten is utterly and perfectly to seize, and hold him in his eternal integrity —robes, ashes, and sting.

Again: the merchant says, "He that oppresseth the poor to increase his riches, shall surely come to want." And again, more strongly: "Rob not the poor because he is poor; neither oppress the afflicted in the place of business. For God shall spoil the soul of those that spoiled them."

This "robbing the poor because he is poor," is especially the mercantile form of theft, consisting in taking advantage of a man's necessities in order to obtain his labor or property at a reduced price. The ordinary highwayman's opposite form of robbery—of the rich, because he is rich—does not appear to occur so often to the old merchant's mind; probably because, being less profitable and more dangerous than the robbery of the poor, it is rarely practiced by persons of discretion.

But the two most remarkable passages in their deep general significance are the following :—

"The rich and the poor have met. God is their maker. "The rich and the poor have met. God is their light." They "have met:" more literally, have stood in each other's way (*obviaverunt*). That is to say, as long as the world lasts, the action and counteraction of wealth and poverty, the meeting, face to face, of rich and poor, is just as appointed and necessary a law of that world as the flow of stream to sea, or the interchange of power among the electric clouds:—"God is their maker." But, also, this action may be either gentle and just, or convulsive and destructive: it may be by rage of devouring flood, or by lapse of serviceable wave;—in blackness of thunderstroke, or continual force of vital fire, soft, and shapeable into love-syllables from far away. And which of these it shall be depends on both rich and poor knowing that God is their light; that in the mystery of human life there is no other light than this by which they can see each other's faces, and live;—light, which is called in another of the books among which the merchant's maxims have been preserved, the "sun of justice,"* of which it is promised that it shall rise at last with "healing" (health-giving or helping, making whole or setting at one) in its wings. For truly

---

*More accurately, Sun of Justness; but instead of the harsh word "Justness," the old English "Righteousness" being commonly employed, has, by getting confused with "godliness," or attracting about it various vague and broken meanings, prevented most persons from receiving the force of the passages in which it occurs. The word "righteousness" properly refers to the justice of rule, or right, as distinguished from "equity," which refers to the justice of balance. More broadly, Righteousness is King's justice; and Equity, Judge's justice; the King guiding or ruling all, the Judge dividing or discerning between opposites (therefore, the double question, "Man, who made me a ruler—δικαστής—or a divider—μεριστής—over you?") Thus, with respect to the Justice of Choice (selection, the feebler and passive justice), we have from lego,—lex, legal, loi, and loyal; and with respect to the Justice of Rule (direction, the stronger and active justice), we have from rego, —rex, regal, roi, and royal.

this healing is only possible by means of justice; no love, no faith, no hope will do it; men will be unwisely fond—vainly faithful, unless primarily they are just; and the mistake of the best men through generation after generation, has been that great one of thinking to help the poor by almsgiving, and by preaching of patience or of hope, and by every other means, emollient or consolatory, except the one thing which God orders for them, justice. But this justice, with its accompanying holiness or helpfulness, being even by the best men denied in its trial time, is by the mass of men hated wherever it appears: so that, when the choice was one day fairly put to them, they denied the Helpful One and the Just;* and desired a murderer, sedition-raiser, and robber, to be granted to them;—the murderer instead of the Lord of Life, the sedition-raiser instead of the Prince of Peace, and the robber instead of the Just Judge of all the world.

I have just spoken of the flowing of streams to the sea as a partial image of the action of wealth. In one respect it is not a partial, but a perfect image. The popular economist thinks himself wise in having discovered that wealth, or the forms of property in general, must go where they are required; that where demand is, supply must follow. He further declares that this course of demand and supply cannot be forbidden by human laws. Precisely in the same sense, and with the same certainty, the waters of the world go where they are required. Where the land falls, the water flows. The course neither of clouds nor rivers can be forbidden by human will. But the disposition and administration of them can be altered by human forethought. Whether the stream shall be a curse or a blessing,

---

*In another place written, with the same meaning, "Just, and having salvation."

depends upon man's labor, and administrating intelligence. For centuries after centuries, great districts of the world, rich in soil, and favored in climate, have lain desert under the rage of their own rivers; not only desert, but plague-struck. The stream which, rightly directed, would have flowed in soft irrigation from field to field—would have purified the air, given food to man and beast, and carried their burdens for them on its bosom—now overwhelms the plain, and poisons the wind; its breath pestilence, and its work famine. In like manner this wealth "goes where it is required." No human laws can withstand its flow. They can only guide it: but this, the leading trench and limiting mound can do so thoroughly, that it shall become water of life—the riches of the hand of wisdom;* or, on the contrary, by leaving it to its own lawless flow, they may make it, what it has been too often, the last and deadliest of national plagues: water of Marah—the water which feeds the roots of all evil.

The necessity of these laws of distribution or restraint is curiously overlooked in the ordinary political economist's definition of his own "science." He calls it, shortly, the "science of getting rich." But there are many sciences, as well as many arts, of getting rich. Poisoning people of large estates, was one employed largely in the middle ages; adulteration of food of people of small estates, is one employed largely now. The ancient and honorable Highland method of blackmail; the more modern and less honorable system of obtaining goods on credit, and the other variously improved methods of appropriation—which, in major and minor scales of industry, down to the most artistic pocket-picking, we owe to recent genius,

---

* "Length of days in her right hand; in her left, riches and honor."

—all come under the general head of sciences, or arts, of getting rich.

So that it is clear the popular economist, in calling his science the science *par excellence* of getting rich, must attach some peculiar ideas of limitation to its character. I hope I do not misrepresent him, by assuming that he means *his* science to be the science of "getting rich by legal or just means." In this definition, is the word "just," or "legal," finally to stand? For it is possible among certain nations, or under certain rulers, or by help of certain advocates, that proceedings may be legal which are by no means just. If, therefore, we leave at last only the word "just" in that place of our definition, the insertion of this solitary and small word will make a notable difference in the grammar of our science. For then it will follow that, in order to grow rich scientifically, we must grow rich justly; and, therefore, know what is just; so that our economy will no longer depend merely on prudence, but on jurisprudence—and that of divine, not human law. Which prudence is indeed of no mean order, holding itself, as it were, high in the air of heaven, and gazing forever on the light of the sun of justice; hence the souls which have excelled in it are represented by Dante as stars forming in heaven forever the figure of the eye of an eagle: they having been in life the discerners of light from darkness; or to the whole human race, as the light of the body, which is the eye; while those souls which form the wings of the bird (giving power and dominion to justice, "healing in its wings") trace also in light the inscription in heaven: "DILIGITE JUSTITIAM QUI JUDICATIS TERRAM." "Ye who judge the earth, give" (not, observe, merely love, but) "diligent love to justice:" the love which seeks diligently, that is to say, choosingly, and by preference to all things else. Which judging or doing judgment in the earth is, according to their capacity and position, required not of judges only, nor of rulers only, but of all men :* a truth sorrowfully lost sight of even by those who are ready enough to apply to themselves passages in which Christian men are spoken of as called to be "saints" (*i. e.* to helpful or healing functions); and "chosen to be kings" (*i. e.* to knowing or directing functions); the true meaning of these titles having been long lost through the pretences of unhelpful and unable persons to saintly and kingly character; also through the once popular idea that both the sanctity and royalty are to consist in wearing long robes and high crowns, instead of in mercy and judgment; whereas all true sanctity is saving power, as all true royalty is ruling power; and injustice is part and parcel of the denial of such power, which "makes men as the creeping things, as the fishes of the sea, that have no ruler over them." †

Absolute justice is indeed no more attainable than absolute truth; but the righteous man is distinguished from the unrighteous by his desire and hope of justice, as the true man from the false by his desire and hope of truth. And though absolute justice be unattainable, as much

---

* I hear that several of our lawyers have been greatly amused by the statement in the first of these papers that a lawyer's function was to do justice. I do not intend it for a jest; nevertheless it will be seen that in the above passage neither the determination nor doing of justice are contemplated as functions wholly peculiar to the lawyer. Possibly, the more our standing armies, whether of soldiers, pastors, or legislators (the generic term "pastor" including all teachers, and the generic term "lawyer" including makers as well as interpreters of law), can be superseded by the force of national-heroism, wisdom, and honesty, the better it may be for the nation.

† It being the privilege of the fishes, as it is of rats and wolves, to live by the laws of demand and supply; but the distinction of humanity, to live by those of right.

justice as we need for all practical use is attainable by all those who make it their aim.

We have to examine, then, in the subject before us, what are the laws of justice respecting payment of labor—no small part, these, of the foundations of all jurisprudence.

I reduced, in my last paper, the idea of money payment to its simplest or radical terms. In those terms its nature, and the conditions of justice respecting it, can be best ascertained.

Money payment, as there stated, consists radically in a promise to some person working for us, that for the time and labor he spends in our service to-day we will give or procure equivalent time and labor in his service at any future time when he may demand it.*

If we promise to give him less labor than he has given us, we under-pay him. If we promise to give him more labor than he has given us, we over-pay him. In practice, according to the laws of demand and supply, when two men are ready to do the work, and only one man wants to have it done, the two men underbid each other for it; and the one who gets it to do, is under-paid. But when two men want the work done, and there is only one man ready to do it, the two men who want it done over-bid each other, and the workman is over-paid.

I will examine these two points of injustice in succes-

---

* It might appear at first that the market price of labor expressed such an exchange: but this is a fallacy, for the market price is the momentary price of the kind of labor required, but the just price is its equivalent of the productive labor of mankind. This difference will be analyzed in its place. It must be noted also that I speak here only of the exchangeable value of labor, not of that of commodities. The exchangeable value of a commodity is that of the labor required to produce it, multiplied into the force of the demand for it. If the value of the labor $= x$ and the force of the demand $= y$, the exchangeable value of the commodity is xy, in which if either $x = 0$, or $y = 0$, $xy = 0$.

sion; but first I wish the reader clearly to understand the central principle, lying between the two, of right or just payment.

When we ask a service of any man, he may either give it us freely, or demand payment for it. Respecting free gift of service, there is no question at present, that being a matter of affection—not of traffic. But if he demand payment for it, and we wish to treat him with absolute equity, it is evident that this equity can only consist in giving time for time, strength for strength, and skill for skill. If a man works an hour for us, and we only promise to work half-an-hour for him in return, we obtain an unjust advantage. If, on the contrary, we promise to work an hour and a half for him in return, he has an unjust advantage. The justice consists in absolute exchange; or, if there be any respect to the stations of the parties, it will not be in favor of the employer; there is certainly no equitable reason in a man's being poor, that if he give me a pound of bread to-day, I should return him less than a pound of bread to-morrow; or any equitable reason in a man's being uneducated, that if he uses a certain quantity of skill and knowledge in my service, I should use a less quantity of skill and knowledge in his. Perhaps, ultimately, it may appear desirable, or, to say the least, gracious, that I should give in return somewhat more than I received. But at present, we are concerned on the law of justice only, which is that of perfect and accurate exchange;—one circumstance only interfering with the simplicity of this radical idea of just payment—that inasmuch as labor (rightly directed) is fruitful just as seed is, the fruit (or "interest," as it is called) of the labor first given, or "advanced," ought to be taken into account, and balanced by an additional quantity of labor in the subsequent repayment. Supposing the repayment to take place at the end of a year, or of any other given time, this calculation could be approximately made; but as money (that is to say, cash) payment involves no reference to time (it being optional with the person paid to spend what he receives at once or after any number of years), we can only assume, generally, that some slight advantage must in equity be allowed to the person who advances the labor, so that the typical form of bargain will be: If you give me an hour to-day, I will give you an hour and five minutes on demand. If you give me a pound of bread to-day, I will give you seventeen ounces on demand, and so on. All that it is necessary for the reader to note is, that the amount returned is at least in equity not to be *less* than the amount given.

The abstract idea, then, of just or due wages, as respects the laborer, is that they will consist in a sum of money which will at any time procure for him at least as much labor as he has given, rather more than less. And this equity or justice of payment is, observe, wholly independent of any reference to the number of men who are willing to do the work. I want a horseshoe for my horse. Twenty smiths, or twenty thousand smiths, may be ready to forge it; their number does not in one atom's weight affect the question of the equitable payment of the one who *does* forge it. It costs him a quarter of an hour of his life, and so much skill and strength of arm to make that horseshoe for me. Then at some future time I am bound in equity to give a quarter of an hour, and some minutes more, of my life (or of some other person's at my disposal), and also as much strength of arm and skill, and a little more, in making or doing what the smith may have need of.

Such being the abstract theory of just remunerative payment, its application is practically modified by the fact that the order for labor, given in payment, is general, while labor received is special. The current coin or document is practically an order on the nation for so much work of any kind; and this universal applicability to immediate need renders it so much more valuable than special labor can be, that an order for a less quantity of this general toil will always be accepted as a just equivalent for a greater quantity of special toil. Any given craftsman will always be willing to give an hour of his own work in order to receive command over half-an-hour, or even much less, of national work. This source of uncertainty, together with the difficulty of determining the monetary value of skill,*

---

*Under the term "skill" I mean to include the united force of experience, intellect, and passion in their operation on manual labor : and under the term "passion," to include the entire range and agency of the moral feelings ; from the simple patience and gentleness of mind which will give continuity and fineness to the touch, or enable one person to work without fatigue, and with good effect, twice as long as another, up-to the qualities of character which render science possible—(the retardation of science by envy is one of the most tremendous losses in the economy of the present century)—and to the incommunicable emotion and imagination which are the first and mightiest sources of all value in art.

It is highly singular that political economists should not yet have perceived, if not the moral, at least the passionate element, to be an inextricable quantity in every calculation. I cannot conceive, for instance, how it was possible that Mr. Mill should have followed the true clue so far as to write,—"No limit can be set to the importance—even in a purely productive and material point of view—of mere thought," without seeing that it was logically necessary to add also, "and of mere feeling." And this the more, because in his first definition of labor he includes in the idea of it "all feelings of a disagreeable kind connected with the employment of one's thoughts in a particular occupation." True ; but why not also, "feelings of an agreeable kind?" It can hardly be supposed that the feelings which retard labor are more essentially a part of the labor than those which accelerate it. The first are paid for as pain, the second as power. The workman is merely indemnified for the first ; but the second both produce a part of the exchangeable value of the work, and materially increase its actual quantity.

"Fritz is with us. *He* is worth fifty thousand men." Truly, a large addition to the material force;—consisting, however, be it

renders the ascertainment (even approximate) of the proper wages of any given labor in terms of a currency, matter of considerable complexity. But they do not affect the principle of exchange. The worth of the work may not be easily known; but it *has* a worth, just as fixed and real as the specific gravity of a substance, though such specific gravity may not be easily ascertainable when the substance is united with many others. Nor is there any difficulty or chance in determining it as in determining the ordinary maxima and minima of vulgar political economy. There are few bargains in which the buyer can ascertain with anything like precision that the seller would have taken no less;—or the seller acquire more than a comfortable faith that the purchaser would have given no more. This impossibility of precise knowledge prevents neither from striving to attain the desired point of greatest vexation and injury to the other, nor from accepting it for a scientific principle that he is to buy for the least and sell for the most possible, though what the real least or most may be he cannot tell. In like manner, a just person lays it down for a scientific principle that he is to pay a just price, and, without being able precisely to ascertain the limits of such a price, will nevertheless strive to attain the closest possible approximation to them. A practically serviceable approximation he *can* obtain. It is easier to determine scientifically what a man ought to have for his work, than what his necessities will compel him to take for it. His necessities can only be ascertained by empirical, but his due by analytical investiga-

---

observed, not more in operations carried on in Fritz's head, than in operations carried on in his armies' heart. "No limit can be set to the importance of *mere* thought." Perhaps not! Nay, suppose some day it should turn out that "mere" thought was in itself a recommendable object of production, and that all Material production was only a step toward this more precious Immaterial one?

tion. In the one case, you try your answer to the sum like a puzzled schoolboy—till you find one that fits; in the other, you bring out your result within certain limits, by process of calculation.

Supposing, then, the just wages of any quantity of given labor to have been ascertained, let us examine the first results of just and unjust payment, when in favor of the purchaser or employer; *i.e.* when two men are ready to do the work, and only one wants to have it done.

The unjust purchaser forces the two to bid against each other till he has reduced their demand to its lowest terms. Let us assume that the lowest bidder offers to do the work at half its just price.

The purchaser employs him, and does not employ the other. The first or *apparent* result is, therefore, that one of the two men is left out of employ, or to starvation, just as definitely as by the just procedure of giving fair price to the best workman. The various writers who endeavored to invalidate the positions of my first paper never saw this, and assumed that the unjust hirer employed *both*. He employs both no more than the just hirer. The only difference (in the outset) is that the just man pays sufficiently, the unjust man insufficiently, for the labor of the single person employed.

I say, "in the outset;" for this first or apparent difference is not the actual difference. By the unjust procedure, half the proper price of the work is left in the hands of the employer. This enables him to hire another man at the same unjust rate, on some other kind of work; and the final result is that he has two men working for him at half price, and two are out of employ.

By the just procedure, the whole price of the first piece of work goes in the hands of the man who does it. No surplus being left in the employer's hands, *he* cannot hire another man for another piece of labor. But by precisely so much as his power is diminished, the hired workman's power is increased; that is to say, by the additional half of the price he has received; which additional half *he* has the power of using to employ another man in *his* service. I will suppose, for the moment, the least favorable, though quite probable, case—that, though justly treated himself, he yet will act unjustly to his subordinate; and hire at half-price, if he can. The final result will then be, that one man works for the employer, at just price; one for the workman, at half-price; and two, as in the first case, are still out of employ. These two, as I said before, are out of employ in *both* cases. The difference between the just and unjust procedure does not lie in the number of men hired, but in the price paid to them, and the *persons by whom* it is paid. The essential difference, that which I want the reader to see clearly, is, that in the unjust case, two men work for one, the first hirer. In the just case, one man works for the first hirer, one for the person hired, and so on, down or up through the various grades of service; the influence being carried forward by justice, and arrested by injustice. The universal and constant action of justice in this matter is, therefore, to diminish the power of wealth, in the hands of one individual, over masses of men, and to distribute it through a chain of men. The actual power exerted by the wealth is the same in both cases; but by injustice it is put all in one man's hands, so that he directs at once and with equal force the labor of a circle of men about him; by the just procedure, he is permitted to touch the nearest only, through whom, with diminished force, modified by new minds, the energy of the wealth passes on to others, and so till it exhausts itself.

The immediate operation of justice in this respect is, therefore, to diminish the power of wealth, first in acquisition of luxury, and, secondly, in exercise of moral influence. The employer cannot concentrate so multitudinous labor on his own interests, nor can he subdue so multitudinous mind to his own will. But the secondary operation of justice is not less important. The insufficient payment of the group of men working for one, places each under a maximum of difficulty in rising above his position. The tendency of the system is to check advancement. But the sufficient or just payment, distributed through a descending series of offices or grades of labor,* gives each subordinated person fair and sufficient means of rising in the social scale, if he chooses to use them; and thus not only diminishes the immediate power of wealth, but removes the worst disabilities of poverty.

---

*I am sorry to lose time by answering, however curtly, the equivocations of the writers who sought to obscure the instances given of regulated labor in the first of these papers, by confusing kinds, ranks, and quantities of labor with its qualities. I never said that a colonel should have the same pay as a private, nor a bishop the same pay as a curate. Neither did I say that more work ought to be paid as less work (so that the curate of a parish of two thousand souls should have no more than the curate of a parish of five hundred). But I said that, so far as you employ it at all, bad work should be paid no less than good work; as a bad clergyman yet takes his tithes, a bad physician takes his fee, and a bad lawyer his costs. And this, as will be further shown in the conclusion, I said, and say, partly because the best work never was nor ever will be, done for money at all; but chiefly because, the moment people know they have to pay the bad and good alike, they will try to discern the one from the other, and not use the bad. A sagacious writer in the *Scotsman* asks me if I should like any common scribbler to be paid by Messrs. Smith, Elder and Co. as their good authors are. I should, if they employed him—but would seriously recommend them, for the scribbler's sake, as well as their own, *not* to employ him. The quantity of its money which the country at present invests in scribbling is not, in the outcome of it, economically spent; and even the highly ingenious person to whom this question occurred, might perhaps have been more beneficially employed than in printing it.

It is on this vital problem that the entire destiny of the laborer is ultimately dependent. Many minor interests may sometimes appear to interfere with it, but all branch from it. For instance, considerable agitation is often caused in the minds of the lower classes when they discover the share which they nominally, and, to all appearance, actually, pay out of their wages in taxation (I believe thirty-five or forty per cent.). This sounds very grievous; but in reality the laborer does not pay it, but his employer. If the workman had not to pay it, his wages would be less by just that sum: competition would still reduce them to the lowest rate at which life was possible. Similarly the lower orders agitated for the repeal of the corn laws,* thinking they

---

* I have to acknowledge an interesting communication on the subject of free-trade from Paisley (for a short letter from "A Wellwisher" at——, my thanks are yet more due). But the Scottish writer will, I fear, be disagreeably surprised to hear, that I am, and always have been, an utterly fearless and unscrupulous free-trader. Seven years ago, speaking of the various signs of infancy in the European mind (*Stones of Venice*, vol. iii., p. 168), I wrote: "The first principles of commerce were acknowledged by the English parliament only a few months ago, and in its free-trade measures, and are still so little understood by the million, that *no nation dares to abolish its custom-houses.*"

It will be observed that I do not admit even the idea of reciprocity. Let other nations, if they like, keep their ports shut; every wise nation will throw its own open. It is not the opening them, but a sudden, inconsiderate, and blunderingly experimental manner of opening them, which does the harm. If you have been protecting a manufacture for long series of years, you must not take protection off in a moment, so as to throw every one of its operatives at once out of employ, any more than you must take all its wrappings off a feeble child at once in cold weather, though the cumber of them may have been radically injuring its health. Little by little, you must restore it to freedom and to air.

Most people's minds are in curious confusion on the subject of free trade, because they suppose it to imply enlarged competition. "Protection" (among various other mischievous functions) endeavors to enable one country to compete with another in the production of an article at a disadvantage. When trade is entirely free, no country can be competed with in the articles for the production of which it is naturally calculated; nor can it compete with any

would be better off if bread were cheaper; never perceiving that as soon as bread was permanently cheaper, wages would permanently fall in precisely that proportion. The corn laws were rightly repealed; not, however, because they directly oppressed the poor, but because they indirectly oppressed them in causing a large quantity of their labor to be consumed unproductively. So also unnecessary taxation oppresses them, through destruction of capital, but the destiny of the poor depends primarily always on this one question of dueness of wages. Their distress (irrespectively of that caused by sloth, minor error, or crime) arises on the grand scale from the two reacting forces of competition and oppression. There is not yet, nor will yet for ages be, any real over-population in the world; but a local over-population, or, more accurately, a degree of population locally unmanageable under existing circumstances for want of forethought and sufficient machinery, necessarily shows itself by pressure of competition; and the taking advantage of this competition by the purchaser to obtain their labor unjustly cheap, consummates at once their suffering and his own; for in this (as I believe in every other kind of slavery) the oppressor suffers at last more than the oppressed, and those magnificent lines of Pope, even in all their force, fall short of the truth—

> "Yet, to be just to these poor men of pelf,
> Each does but HATE HIS NEIGHBOR AS HIMSELF:
> Damned to the mines, an equal fate betides
> The slave that digs it, and the slave that hides."

---

other in the production of articles for which it is not naturally calculated. Tuscany, for instance, cannot compete with England in steel, nor England with Tuscany in oil. They must exchange their steel and oil. Which exchange should be as frank and free as honesty and the sea-winds can make it. Competition, indeed, arises at first, and sharply, in order to prove which is strongest in any given manufacture possible to both; this point once ascertained, competition is at an end.

The collateral and reversionary operations of justice in this matter I shall examine hereafter (it being needful first to define the nature of value); proceeding then to consider within what practical terms a juster system may be established; and ultimately the vexed question of the destinies of the unemployed workmen.* Lest, however, the reader should be alarmed at some of the issues to which our investigations seem to be tending, as if in their bearing against the power of wealth they had something in common with those of Socialism, I wish him to know, in accurate terms, one or two of the main points which I have in view.

Whether Socialism has made more progress among the army and navy (where payment is made on my principles), or among the manufacturing operatives (who are paid on my opponents' principles), I leave it to those opponents to

---

* I should be glad if the reader would first clear the ground for himself so far as to determine whether the difficulty lies in getting the work or getting the pay for it. Does he consider occupation itself to be an expensive luxury, difficult of attainment, of which too little is to be found in the world? or is it rather that, while in the enjoyment even of the most athletic delight, men must nevertheless be maintained, and this maintenance is not always forthcoming? We must be clear on this head before going further, as most people are loosely in the habit of talking of the difficulty of "finding employment." Is it employment that we want to find, or support during employment? Is it idleness we wish to put an end to, or hunger? We have to take up both questions in succession, only not both at the same time. · No doubt that work *is* a luxury, and a very great one. It is, indeed, at once a luxury and a necessity; no man can retain either health of mind or body without it. So profoundly do I feel this, that, as will be seen in the sequel, one of the principal objects I would recommend to benevolent and practical persons, is to induce rich people to seek for a larger quantity of this luxury than they at present possess. Nevertheless, it appears by experience that even this healthiest of pleasures may be indulged in to excess, and that human beings are just as liable to surfeit of labor as to surfeit of meat; so that, as on the one hand, it may be charitable to provide, for some people, lighter dinner, and more work,--for others it may be equally expedient to provide lighter work, and more dinner.

ascertain and declare. Whatever their conclusion may be, I think it necessary to answer for myself only this: that if there be any one point insisted on throughout my works more frequently than another, that one point is the impossibility of Equality. My continual aim has been to show the eternal superiority of some men to others, sometimes even of one man to all others; and to show also the advisability of appointing more such persons or person to guide, to lead, or on occasion even to compel and subdue, their inferiors, according to their own better knowledge and wiser will. My principles of Political Economy were all involved in a single phrase spoken three years ago at Manchester: "Soldiers of the Plowshare as well as soldiers of the Sword:" and they were all summed in a single sentence in the last volume of *Modern Painters*—"Government and coöperation are in all things the Laws of Life; Anarchy and competition the Laws of Death."

And with respect to the mode in which these general principles affect the secure possession of property, so far am I from invalidating such security, that the whole gist of these papers will be found ultimately to aim at an extension in its range; and whereas it has long been known and declared that the poor have no right to the property of the rich, I wish it also to be known and declared that the rich have no right to the property of the poor.

But that the working of the system which I have undertaken to develop would in many ways shorten the apparent and direct, though not the unseen and collateral, power, both of wealth, as the Lady of Pleasure, and of capital as the Lord of Toil, I do not deny: on the contrary, I affirm it in all joyfulness; knowing that the attraction of riches is already too strong, as their authority is already too weighty, for the reason of mankind. I said in my last paper that nothing in history had ever been so disgraceful to human intellect as the acceptance among us of the common doctrines of political economy as a science. I have many grounds for saying this, but one of the chief may be given in few words. I know no previous instance in history of a nation's establishing a systematic disobedience to the first principles of its professed religion. The writings which we (verbally) esteem as divine, not only denounce the love of money as the source of all evil, and as an idolatry abhorred of the Deity, but declare mammon service to be the accurate and irreconcilable opposite of God's service: and, whenever they speak of riches absolute, and poverty absolute, declare woe to the rich, and blessing to the poor. Whereupon we forthwith investigate a science of becoming rich, as the shortest road to national prosperity.

"Tai Cristian dannerà l'Etiòpe,
Quando si partiranno i due collegi,
L'UNO IN ETERNO RICCO, E L'ALTRO INÒPE."

ESSAY IV.

AD VALOREM.

IN the last paper we saw that just payment of labor consisted in a sum of money which would approximately obtain equivalent labor at a future time: we have now to examine the means of obtaining such equivalence. Which question involves the definition of Value, Wealth, Price, and Produce.

None of these terms are yet defined so as to be understood by the public. But the last, Produce, which one might have thought the clearest of all, is, in use, the most ambiguous; and the examination of the kind of ambiguity attendant on its present employment will best open the way to our work.

In his chapter on Capital,* Mr. J. S. Mill instances, as a capitalist, a hardware manufacturer, who, having intended to spend a certain portion of the proceeds of his business in buying plate and jewels, changes his mind, and "pays it as wages to additional workpeople." The effect is stated by Mr. Mill to be, that "more food is appropriated to the consumption of productive laborers."

Now, I do not ask, though, had I written this paragraph, it would surely have been asked of me, What is to become of the silversmiths? If they are truly unproductive persons, we will acquiesce in their extinction. And though in

---

* Book I., chap. iv., s. 1. To save space, my future references to Mr. Mill's work will be by numerals only, as in this instance, I. iv. 1. Ed. in 2 vols. 8vo. Parker, 1848.

another part of the same passage, the hardware merchant is supposed also to dispense with a number of servants, whose "food is thus set free for productive purposes," I do not inquire what will be the effect, painful or otherwise, upon the servants, of this emmacipation of their food. But I very seriously inquire why ironware is produce, and silverware is not? That the merchant consumes the one, and sells the other, certainly does not constitute the difference, unless it can be shown (which, indeed, I perceive it to be becoming daily more and more the aim of tradesmen to show) that commodities are made to be sold, and not to be consumed. The merchant is an agent of conveyance to the consumer in one case, and is himself the consumer in the other :* but the laborers are in either case equally productive, since they have produced goods to the same value, if the hardware and the plate are both goods.

And what distinction separates them? It is indeed possible that in the "comparative estimate of the moralist," with which Mr. Mill says political economy has nothing to do (III. i. 2) a steel fork might appear a more substantial production than a silver one: we may grant also that knives, no less than forks, are good produce; and scythes and plowshares serviceable articles. But, how of bayonets? Supposing the hardware merchant to effect large sales of

---

* If Mr. Mill had wished to show the difference in result between consumption and sale, he should have represented the hardware merchant as consuming his own goods instead of selling them; similarly, the silver merchant as consuming his own goods instead of selling them. Had he done this, he would have made his position clearer, though less tenable; and perhaps this was the position he really intended to take, tacitly involving his theory, elsewhere stated, and shown in the sequel of this paper to be false, that demand for commodities is not demand for labor. But by the most diligent scrutiny of the paragraph now under examination, I cannot determine whether it is a fallacy pure and simple, or the half of one fallacy supported by the whole of a greater one ; so that I treat it here on the kinder assumption that it is one fallacy only.

these, by help of the "setting free" of the food of his servants and his silversmith,—is he still employing productive laborers, or, in Mr. Mill's words, laborers who increase "the stock of permanent means of enjoyment" (I. iii. 4). Or if, instead of bayonets, he supply bombs, will not the absolute and final "enjoyment" of even these energetically productive articles (each of which costs ten pounds)* be dependent on a proper choice of time and place for their *enfantement;* choice, that is to say, depending on those philosophical considerations with which political economy has nothing to do?†

I should have regretted the need of pointing out inconsistency in any portion of Mr. Mill's work, had not the value of his work proceeded from its inconsistencies. He deserves honor among economists by inadvertently disclaiming the principles which he states, and tacitly introducing the moral considerations with which he declares his science has no connection. Many of his chapters are, therefore, true and valuable; and the only conclusions of his which I have to dispute are those which follow from his premises.

Thus, the idea which lies at the root of the passage we have just been examining, namely, that labor applied to produce luxuries will not support so many persons as labor applied to produce useful articles, is entirely true; but the instance given fails—and in four directions of failure at

---

* I take Mr. Helps' estimate in his essay on War.

† Also when the wrought silver vases of Spain were dashed to fragments by our custom-house officers, because bullion might be imported free of duty, but not brains, was the axe that broke them productive?—the artist who wrought them unproductive? Or again. If the woodman's axe is productive, is the executioner's? as also, if the hemp of a cable be productive, does not the productiveness of hemp in a halter depend on its moral more than on its material application?

once—because Mr. Mill has not defined the real meaning of usefulness. The definition which he has given—"capacity to satisfy a desire, or serve a purpose" (III. i. 2)—applies equally to the iron and silver; while the true definition—which he has not given, but which nevertheless underlies the false verbal definition in his mind, and comes out once or twice by accident (as in the words "any support to life or strength" in I. i. 5)—applies to some articles of iron, but not to others, and to some articles of silver, but not to others. It applies to plows, but not to bayonets; and to forks, but not to filigree.*

The eliciting of the true definition will give us the reply to our first question, "What is value?" respecting which, however, we must first hear the popular statements.

"The word 'value,' when used without adjunct, always means, in political economy, value in exchange" (Mill, III. i. 3). So that, if two ships cannot exchange their rudders, their rudders are, in politico-economic language, of no value to either.

But "the subject of political economy is wealth."—(Preliminary remarks, page 1.)

And wealth "consists of all useful and agreeable objects which possess exchangeable value."—(Preliminary remarks, page 10.)

It appears, then, according to Mr. Mill, that usefulness and agreeableness underlie the exchange value, and must be ascertained to exist in the thing, before we can esteem it an object of wealth.

Now, the economical usefulness of a thing depends not merely on its own nature, but on the number of people who can and will use it. A horse is useless, and therefore

---

* Filigree: that is to say, generally, ornament dependent on complexity, not on art.

unsaleable, if no one can ride,—a sword if no one can strike, and meat, if no one can eat. Thus every material utility depends on its relative human capacity.

Similarly: The agreeableness of a thing depends not merely on its own likeableness, but on the number of people who can be got to like it. The relative agreeableness, and therefore saleableness, of "a pot of the smallest ale," and of "Adonis painted by a running brook," depends virtually on the opinion of Demos, in the shape of Christopher Sly. That is to say, the agreeableness of a thing depends on its relative human disposition.* Therefore, political economy, being a science of wealth, must be a science respecting human capacities and dispositions. But moral considerations have nothing to do with political economy (III. i. 2). Therefore, moral considerations have nothing to do with human capacities and dispositions.

I do not wholly like the look of this conclusion from Mr. Mill's statements:—let us try Mr. Ricardo's.

"Utility is not the measure of exchangeable value, though it is absolutely essential to it."—(Chap. I. sect. i.)

---

*These statements sound crude in their brevity; but will be found of the utmost importance when they are developed. Thus, in the above instance, economists have never perceived that disposition to buy is a wholly *moral* element in demand: that is to say, when you give a man half-a-crown, it depends on his disposition whether he is rich or poor with it—whether he will buy disease, ruin, and hatred, or buy health, advancement, and domestic love. And thus the agreeableness or exchange value of every offered commodity depends on production, not merely of the commodity, but of buyers of it; therefore on the education of buyers and on all the moral elements by which their disposition to buy this, or that, is formed. I will illustrate and expand into final consequences every one of these definitions in its place: at present they can only be given with extremest brevity; for in order to put the subject at once in a connected form before the reader, I have thrown into one, the opening definitions of four chapters; namely, of that on Value ("Ad Valorem"); on Price ("Thirty Pieces"); on Production ("Demeter"); and on Economy ("The Law of the House").

Essential in what degree, Mr. Ricardo? There may be greater and less degrees of utility. Meat, for instance, may be so good as to be fit for any one to eat, or so bad as to be fit for no one to eat. What is the exact degree of goodness which is "essential" to its exchangeable value, but not "the measure" of it? How good must the meat be, in order to possess any exchangeable value; and how bad must it be—(I wish this were a settled question in London markets)—in order to possess none?

There appears to be some hitch, I think, in the working even of Mr. Ricardo's principles; but let him take his own example. "Suppose that in the early stages of society the bows and arrows of the hunter were of equal value with the implements of the fisherman. Under such circumstances the value of the deer, the produce of the hunter's day's labor, would be *exactly*" (italics mine) "equal to the value of the fish, the product of the fisherman's day's labor. The comparative value of the fish and game would be *entirely* regulated by the quantity of labor realized in each." (Ricardo, chap. iii. On Value).

Indeed! Therefore, if the fisherman catches one sprat, and the huntsman one deer, one sprat will be equal in value to one deer; but if the fisherman catches no sprat, and the huntsman two deer, no sprat will be equal in value to two deer?

Nay; but—Mr. Ricardo's supporters may say—he means, on an average;—if the average product of a day's work of fisher and hunter be one fish and one deer, the one fish will always be equal in value to the one deer.

Might I inquire the species of fish. Whale? or whitebait? *

---

* Perhaps it may be said, in further support of Mr. Ricardo, that he meant, "when the utility is constant or given, the price varies as

It would be waste of time to pursue these fallacies further; we will seek for a true definition.

Much store has been set for centuries upon the use of our English classical education. It were to be wished that our well-educated merchants recalled to mind always this much of their Latin schooling,—that the nominative of *valorem* (a word already sufficiently familiar to them) is

---

the quantity of labor." If he meant this, he should have said it; but, had he meant it, he could have hardly missed the necessary result, that utility would be one measure of price (which he expressly denies it to be); and that, to prove saleableness, he had to prove a given quantity of utility, as well as a given quantity of labor; to wit, in his own instance, that the deer and fish would each feed the same number of men, for the same number of days, with equal pleasure to their palates. The fact is, he did not know what he meant himself. The general idea which he had derived from commercial experience, without being able to analyze it, was, that when the demand is constant, the price varies as the quantity of labor required for production; or,—using the formula I gave in last paper—when y is constant, $x\,y$ varies as x. But demand never is, nor can be, ultimately constant, if x varies distinctly; for, as price rises, consumers fall away; and as soon as there is a monopoly (and all scarcity is a form of monopoly; so that every commodity is affected occasionally by some color of monopoly), y becomes the most influential condition of the price. Thus the price of a painting depends less on its merits than on the interest taken in it by the public; the price of singing less on the labor of the singer than the number of persons who desire to hear him; and the price of gold less on the scarcity which affects it in common with cerium or iridium, than on the sunlight color and unalterable purity by which it attracts the admiration and answers the trusts of mankind.

It must be kept in mind, however, that I use the word "demand" in a somewhat different sense from economists usually. They mean by it "the quantity of a thing sold." I mean by it "the force of the buyer's capable intention to buy." In good English, a person's "demand" signifies, not what he gets, but what he asks for.

Economists also do not notice that objects are not valued by absolute bulk or weight, but by such bulk and weight as is necessary to bring them into use. They say, for instance, that water bears no price in the market. It is true that a cupful does not, but a lake does: just as a handful of dust does not, but an acre does. And were it possible to make even the possession of the cupful or handful permanent (*i. e.* to find a place for them,) the earth and sea would be bought up by handfuls and cupfuls.

valor; a word which, therefore, ought to be familiar to them. *Valor,* from *valere,* to be well, or strong (ὑγιαίνω);— strong, *in* life (if a man), or valiant; strong, *for* life (if a thing), or valuable. To be "valuable," therefore, is to "avail toward life." A truly valuable or availing thing is that which leads to life with its whole strength. In proportion as it does not lead to life, or as its strength is broken, it is less valuable; in proportion as it leads away from life, it is unvaluable or malignant.

The value of a thing, therefore, is independent of opinion, and of quantity. Think what you will of it, gain how much you may of it, the value of the thing itself is neither greater nor less. Forever it avails, or avails not; no estimate can raise, no disdain depress, the power which it holds from the Maker of things and of men.

The real science of political economy, which has yet to be distinguished from the bastard science, as medicine from witchcraft, and astronomy from astrology, is that which teaches nations to desire and labor for the things that lead to life; and which teaches them to scorn and destroy the things that lead to destruction. And if, in a state of infancy, they suppose indifferent things, such as excrescences of shell-fish, and pieces of blue and red stone, to be valuable, and spend large measure of the labor which ought to be employed for the extension and ennobling of life, in diving or digging for them, and cutting them into various shapes,— or if, in the same state of infancy, they imagine precious and beneficent things, such as air, light, and cleanliness, to be valueless,—or if, finally, they imagine the conditions of their own existence, by which alone they can truly possess or use anything, such, for instance, as peace, trust, and love, to be prudently exchangeable, when the market offers, for gold, iron, or excrescences of shells—the great and only science of Political Economy teaches them, in all these cases, what is vanity, and what substance; and how the service of Death, the Lord of Waste, and of eternal emptiness, differs from the service of Wisdom, the Lady of Saving, and of eternal fullness; she who has said, "I will cause those that love me to inherit SUBSTANCE; and I will FILL their treasures."

The "Lady of Saving," in a profounder sense than that of the savings' bank, though that is a good one: Madonna della Salute,—Lady of Health—which, though commonly spoken of as if separate from wealth, is indeed a part of wealth. This word, "wealth," it will be remembered, is the next we have to define.

"To be wealthy," says Mr. Mill, is "to have a large stock of useful articles."

I accept this definition. Only let us perfectly understand it. My opponents often lament my not giving them enough logic: I fear I must at present use a little more than they will like; but this business of Political Economy is no light one, and we must allow no loose terms in it.

We have, therefore, to ascertain in the above definition, first, what is the meaning of "having," or the nature of Possession. Then what is the meaning of "useful," or the nature of Utility.

And first of possession. At the crossing of the transepts of Milan Cathedral has lain, for three hundred years, the embalmed body of St. Carlo Borromeo. It holds a golden crosier, and has a cross of emeralds on its breast. Admitting the crosier and emeralds to be useful articles, is the body to be considered as "having" them? Do they, in the politico-economical sense of property, belong to it? If not, and if we may, therefore, conclude generally that a dead body cannot possess property, what degree and period of animation in the body will render possession possible?

As thus: lately in a wreck of a Californian ship, one of the passengers fastened a belt about him with two hundred pounds of gold in it, with which he was found afterward at the bottom. Now, as he was sinking—had he the gold? or had the gold him?*

And if, instead of sinking him in the sea by its weight, the gold had struck him on the forehead, and thereby caused incurable disease—suppose palsy or insanity,— would the gold in that case have been more a "possession" than in the first? Without pressing the inquiry up through instances of gradual increasing vital power over the gold (which I will, however, give, if they are asked for), I presume the reader will see that possession, or "having," is not an absolute, but a gradated, power; and consists not only in the quantity or nature of the thing possessed, but also (and in a greater degree) in its suitableness to the person possessing it, and in his vital power to use it.

And our definition of Wealth, expanded, becomes: "The possession of useful articles, *which we can use.*" This is a very serious change. For wealth, instead of depending merely on a "have," is thus seen to depend on a "can." Gladiator's death, on a "habet;" but soldier's victory, and state's salvation, on a "quo plurimum posset." (Liv. VII. 6.) And what we reasoned of only as accumulation of material, is seen to demand also accumulation of capacity.

So much for our verb. Next for our adjective. What is the meaning of "useful?"

The inquiry is closely connected with the last. For

---

* Compare George Herbert, *The Church Porch*, Stanza 28.

what is capable of use in the hands of some persons, is capable, in the hands of others, of the opposite of use, called commonly, "from-use or ab-use." And it depends on the person, much more than on the article, whether its usefulness or ab-usefulness will be the quality developed in it. Thus, wine, which the Greeks, in their Bacchus, made, rightly, the type of all passion, and which, when used, "cheereth god and man" (that is to say, strengthens both the divine life, or reasoning power, and the earthly, or carnal power, of man); yet, when abused, becomes "Dionusos," hurtful especially to the divine part of man, or reason. And again, the body itself, being equally liable to use and to abuse, and, when rightly disciplined, serviceable to the State, both for war and labor;—but when not disciplined, or abused, valueless to the State, and capable only of continuing the private or single existence of the individual (and that but feebly)—the Greeks called such a body an "idiotic" or "private" body, from their word signifying a person employed in no way directly useful to the State; whence, finally, our "idiot," meaning a person entirely occupied with his own concerns.

Hence, it follows, that if a thing is to be useful, it must be not only of an availing nature, but in availing hands. Or, in accurate terms, usefulness is value in the hands of the valiant; so that this science of wealth being, as we have just seen, when regarded as the science of Accumulation, accumulative of capacity as well as of material,—when regarded as the Science of Distribution, is distribution not absolute, but discriminate; not of every thing to every man, but of the right thing to the right man. A difficult science, dependent on more than arithmetic.

Wealth, therefore, is "THE POSSESSION OF THE VALUABLE BY THE VALIANT;" and in considering it as a power existing in a nation, the two elements, the value of the thing, and the valor of its possessor, must be estimated together. Whence it appears that many of the persons commonly considered wealthy, are in reality no more wealthy than the locks of their own strong boxes are; they being inherently and eternally incapable of wealth; and operating for the nation, in an economical point of view, either as pools of dead water, and eddies in a stream (which, so long as the stream flows, are useless, or serve only to drown people, but may become of importance in a state of stagnation, should the stream dry); or else, as dams in a river, of which the ultimate service depends not on the dam, but the miller; or else, as mere accidental stays and impediments, acting, not as wealth, but (for we ought to have a correspondent term) as "illth," causing various devastation and trouble around them in all directions; or lastly, act not at all, but are merely animated conditions of delay, (no use being possible of anything they have until they are dead,) in which last condition they are nevertheless often useful *as* delays, and "impedimenta," if a nation is apt to move too fast.

This being so, the difficulty of the true science of Political Economy lies not merely in the need of developing manly character to deal with material value, but in the fact, that while the manly character and material value only form wealth by their conjunction, they have nevertheless a mutually destructive operation on each other. For the manly character is apt to ignore, or even cast away, the material value:—whence that of Pope:—

" Sure, of qualities demanding praise
More go to ruin fortunes, than to raise."

And on the other hand, the material value is apt to undermine the manly character; so that it must be our work, in the issue, to examine what evidence there is of the effect of wealth on the minds of its possessors; also, what kind of person it is who usually sets himself to obtain wealth, and succeeds in doing so; and whether the world owes more gratitude to rich or to poor men, either for their moral influence upon it, or for chief goods, discoveries, and practical advancements. I may, however, anticipate future conclusion so far as to state that in a community regulated only by laws of demand and supply, and protected from open violence, the persons who become rich are, generally speaking, industrious, resolute, proud, covetous, prompt, methodical, sensible, unimaginative, insensitive, and ignorant. The persons who remain poor are the entirely foolish, the entirely wise,* the idle, the reckless, the humble, the thoughtful, the dull, the imaginative, the sensitive, the well-informed, the improvident, the irregularly and impulsively wicked, the clumsy knave, the open thief, and the entirely merciful, just, and godly person.

Thus far then of wealth. Next, we have to ascertain the nature of PRICE; that is to say, of exchange value, and its expression by currencies.

Note first, of exchange, there can be no *profit* in it. It is only in labor there can be profit—that is to say a "making in advance," or "making in favor of" (from proficio). In exchange, there is only advantage, *i.e.* a bringing of vantage or power to the exchanging persons. Thus, one man, by sowing and reaping, turns one measure of corn into two measures. That is Profit. Another by digging and forging, turns one spade into two spades. That is Profit. But the man who has two measures of corn wants

---

* "ὁ Ζεὺς δήπου πένεται."—*Aris. Plut.*, 582. It would but weaken the grand words to lean on the preceding ones:—"ὅτι τοῦ Πλούτου παρέχω βελτίονας, ἄνδρας, καὶ τὴν γνώμην, καὶ τὴν ἰδέαν."

sometimes to dig; and the man who has two spades wants sometimes to eat:—They exchange the gained grain for the gained tool; and both are the better for the exchange; but though there is much advantage in the transaction, there is no profit. Nothing is constructed or produced. Only that which had been before constructed is given to the person by whom it can be used. If labor is necessary to effect the exchange, that labor is in reality involved in the production, and, like all other labor, bears profit. Whatever number of men are concerned in the manufacture, or in the conveyance, have share in the profit; but neither the manufacture nor the conveyance are the exchange, and in the exchange itself there is no profit.

There may, however, be acquisition, which is a very different thing. If, in the exchange, one man is able to give what cost him little labor for what has cost the other much, he "acquires" a certain quantity of the produce of the other's labor. And precisely what he acquires, the other loses. In mercantile language, the person who thus acquires is commonly said to have "made a profit;" and I believe that many of our merchants are seriously under the impression that it is possible for everybody, somehow, to make a profit in this manner. Whereas, by the unfortunate constitution of the world we live in, the laws both of matter and motion have quite rigorously forbidden universal acquisition of this kind. Profit, or material gain, is attainable only by construction or by discovery; not by exchange. Whenever material gain follows exchange, for every *plus* there is precisely equal *minus*.

Unhappily for the progress of the science of Political Economy, the plus quantities, or,—if I may be allowed to coin an awkward plural—the pluses, make a very positive and venerable appearance in the world, so that every one is eager to learn the science which produces results so magnificent; whereas the minuses have, on the other hand, a tendency to retire into back streets, and other places of shade,—or even to get themselves wholly and finally put out of sight in graves: which renders the algebra of this science peculiar, and difficultly legible: a large number of its negative signs being written by the account-keeper in a kind of red ink, which starvation thins, and makes strangely pale, or even quite invisible ink, for the present.

The Science of Exchange, or, as I hear it has been proposed to call it, of "Catallactics," considered as one of gain, is, therefore, simply nugatory; but considered as one of acquisition, it is a very curious science, differing in its data and basis from every other science known. Thus:— If I can exchange a needle with a savage for a diamond, my power of doing so depends either on the savage's ignorance of social arrangements in Europe, or on his want of power to take advantage of them, by selling the diamond to any one else for more needles. If, further, I make the bargain as completely advantageous to myself as possible, by giving to the savage a needle with no eye in it (reaching, thus, a sufficiently satisfactory type of the perfect operation of catallactic science), the advantage to me in the entire transaction depends wholly upon the ignorance, powerlessness, or heedlessness of the person dealt with. Do away with these, and catallactic advantage becomes impossible. So far, therefore, as the science of exchange relates to the advantage of one of the exchanging persons only, it is founded on the ignorance or incapacity of the opposite person. Where these vanish, it also vanishes. It is, therefore, a science founded on nescience, and an art founded on artlessness. But all other sciences and arts, except this, have for their object the doing away with their opposite nescience and artlessness. *This* science, alone of sciences, must, by all available means, promulgate and prolong its opposite nescience; otherwise the science itself is impossible. It is, therefore, peculiarly and alone, the science of darkness; probably a bastard science—not by any means a *divina scientia*, but one begotten of another father, that father who, advising his children to turn stones into bread, is himself employed in turning bread into stones, and who, if you ask a fish of him (fish not being producible on his estate), can but give you a serpent.

The general law, then, respecting just or economical exchange, is simply this:—There must be advantage on both sides (or if only advantage on one, at least no disadvantage on the other) to the persons exchanging; and just payment for his time, intelligence, and labor, to any intermediate person effecting the transaction (commonly called a merchant): and whatever advantage there is on either side, and whatever pay is given to the intermediate person, should be thoroughly known to all concerned. All attempt at concealment implies some practice of the opposite, or undivine science, founded on nescience. Whence another saying of the Jew merchant's—"As a nail between the stone joints, so doth sin stick fast between buying and selling." Which peculiar riveting of stone and timber, in men's dealings with each other, is again set forth in the house which was to be destroyed—timber and stones together—when Zechariah's roll (more probably "curved sword") flew over it: "the curse that goeth forth over all the earth upon every one that stealeth and holdeth himself guiltless," instantly followed by the vision of the Great Measure;—the measure "of the injustice of them in all the earth" (αὕτη ἡ ἀδικία αὐτῶν ἐν πάσῃ τῇ γῇ), with the weight of lead for its lid, and the woman, the spirit of wickedness, within it ;—that is to say, Wickedness hidden by Dullness, and formalized, outwardly, into ponderously established cruelty. "It shall be set upon its own base in the land of Babel." *

I have hitherto carefully restricted myself, in speaking of exchange, to the use of the term "advantage;" but that term includes two ideas; the advantage, namely, of getting what we *need*, and that of getting what we *wish* for. Three-fourths of the demands existing in the world are romantic; founded on visions, idealisms, hopes, and affections; and the regulation of the purse is, in its essence, regulation of the imagination and the heart. Hence, the right discussion of the nature of price is a very high metaphysical and physical problem; sometimes to be solved only in a passionate manner, as by David in his counting the price of the water of the well by the gate of Bethlehem; but its first conditions are the following:—The price of anything is the quantity of labor given by the person desiring it, in order to obtain possession of it. This price depends on four variable quantities. A. The quantity of wish the purchaser has for the thing; opposed to a, the quantity of wish the seller has to keep it. B. The quantity of labor the purchaser can afford, to obtain the thing; opposed to β, the quantity of labor the seller can afford, to keep it. These quantities are operative only in excess; *i.e.* the quantity of wish (A) means the quantity of wish for this thing, above wish for other things; and the quantity of work (B) means the quantity which can be spared to get this thing from the quantity needed to get other things.

Phenomena of price, therefore, are intensely complex, curious, and interesting—too complex, however, to be

---

*Zech. v. 11. See note on the passage, at page 120.

examined yet; every one of them, when traced far enough, showing itself at last as a part of the bargain of the Poor of the Flock (or "flock of slaughter"), "If ye think good give ME my price, and if not, forbear"—Zech. xi. 12; but as the price of everything is to be calculated finally in labor, it is necessary to define the nature of that standard.

Labor is the contest of the life of man with an opposite; —the term "life" including his intellect, soul, and physical power, contending with question, difficulty, trial, or material force.

Labor is of a higher or lower order, as it includes more or fewer of the elements of life: and labor of good quality, in any kind, includes always as much intellect and feeling as will fully and harmoniously regulate the physical force.

In speaking of the value and price of labor, it is necessary always to understand labor of a given rank and quality, as we should speak of gold or silver of a given standard. Bad (that is, heartless, inexperienced, or senseless) labor cannot be valued; it is like gold of uncertain alloy, or flawed iron.*

The quality and kind of labor being given, its value, like that of all other valuable things, is invariable. But the quantity of it which must be given for other things is variable; and in estimating this variation, the price of

---

* Labor which is entirely good of its kind, that is to say, effective, or efficient, the Greeks called "weighable," or ἄξιος, translated usually "worthy," and because thus substantial and true, they called its price τιμή, the "honorable estimate," of it (honorarium): this word being founded on their conception of true labor as a divine thing, to be honored with the kind of honor given to the gods; whereas the price of false labor, or of that which led away from life, was to be, not honor, but vengeance; for which they reserved another word, attributing the exaction of such price to a peculiar goddess, called Tisiphone, the "requiter (or quittance-taker) of death;" a person versed in the highest branches of arithmetic, and punctual in her habits; with whom accounts current have been opened also in modern days.

other things must always be counted by the quantity of labor; not the price of labor by the quantity of other things.

Thus, if we want to plant an apple sapling in rocky ground, it may take two hours' work; in soft ground, perhaps only half an hour. Grant the soil equally good for the tree in each case. Then the value of the sapling planted by two hours' work is nowise greater than that of the sapling planted in half an hour. One will bear no more fruit than the other. Also, one half-hour of work is as valuable as another half-hour; nevertheless the one sapling has cost four such pieces of work, the other only one. Now the proper statement of this fact is, not that the labor on the hard ground is cheaper than on the soft; but that the tree is dearer. The exchange value may, or may not, afterward depend on this fact. If other people have plenty of soft ground to plant in, they will take no cognizance of our two hours' labor, in the price they will offer for the plant on the rock. And if, through want of sufficient botanical science, we have planted an upas-tree instead of an apple, the exchange-value will be a negative quantity; still less proportionate to the labor expended.

What is commonly called cheapness of labor, signifies, therefore, in reality, that many obstacles have to be overcome by it; so that much labor is required to produce a small result. But this should never be spoken of as cheapness of labor, but as dearness of the object wrought for. It would be just as rational to say that walking was cheap, because we had ten miles to walk home to our dinner, as that labor was cheap, because we had to work ten hours to earn it.

The last word which we have to define is "Production."

I have hitherto spoken of all labor as profitable; because it is impossible to consider under one head the quality or value of labor, and its aim. But labor of the best quality may be various in aim. It may be either constructive ("gathering," from con and struo), as agriculture; nugatory, as jewel-cutting; or destructive ("scattering," from de and struo), as war. It is not, however, always easy to prove labor, apparently nugatory, to be actually so ;* generally, the formula holds good: "he that gathereth not, scattereth;" thus, the jeweler's art is probably very harmful in its ministering to a clumsy and inelegant pride. So that, finally, I believe nearly all labor may be shortly divided into positive and negative labor: positive, that which produces life; negative, that which produces death; the most directly negative labor being murder, and the most directly positive, the bearing and rearing of children; so that in the precise degree which murder is hateful, on the negative side of idleness, in that exact degree child-rearing is admirable, on the positive side of idleness. For which reason, and because of the honor that there is in rearing† children, while the wife is said to

---

* The most accurately nugatory labor is, perhaps, that of which not enough is given to answer a purpose effectually, and which, therefore, has all to be done over again. Also, labor which fails of effect through non-coöperation. The curé of a little village near Bellinzona, to whom I had expressed wonder that the peasants allowed the Ticino to flood their fields, told me that they would not join to build an effectual embankment high up the valley, because everybody said "that would help his neighbors as much as himself." So every proprietor built a bit of low embankment about his own field; and the Ticino, as soon as it had a mind, swept away and swallowed all up together.

† Observe, I say, "rearing," not "begetting." The praise is in the seventh season, not in σπορητός, nor in φυλλαιί, but in ὀπώρα. It is strange that men always praise enthusiastically any person who, by a momentary exertion, saves a life; but praise very hesitatingly a person who, by exertion and self-denial prolonged through years, creates one. We give the crown "ob civem servatum;"—why not "ob civem natum?" Born, I mean, to the full, in soul as well as body. England has oak enough, I think, for both chaplets.

be as the vine (for cheering), the children are as the olive-branch, for praise; nor for praise only, but for peace (because large families can only be reared in times of peace): though since, in their spreading and voyaging in various directions, they distribute strength, they are, to the home strength, as arrows in the hand of a giant—striking here and there, far away.

Labor being thus various in its result, the prosperity of any nation is in exact proportion to the quantity of labor which it spends in obtaining and employing means of life. Observe,—I say, obtaining and employing; that is to say, not merely wisely producing, but wisely distributing and consuming. Economists usually speak as if there were no good in consumption absolute.* So far from this being so, consumption absolute is the end, crown, and perfection of production; and wise consumption is a far more difficult art than wise production. Twenty people can gain money for one who can use it; and the vital question, for individual and for nation, is, never "how much do they make?" but "to what purpose do they spend?"

The reader may, perhaps, have been surprised at the slight reference I have hitherto made to "capital," and its functions. It is here the place to define them.

Capital signifies "head, or source, or root material"— it is material by which some derivative or secondary good, is produced. It is only capital proper (caput vivum, not caput mortuum) when it is thus producing something different from itself. It is a root, which does not enter into vital function till it produces something else than a root; namely, fruit. That fruit will in time again produce roots;

---

*When Mr. Mill speaks of productive consumption, he only means consumption which results in increase of capital, or material wealth. See I. iii. 4, and I. iii. 5.

and so all living capital issues in reproduction of capital; but capital which produces nothing but capital is only root producing root; bulb issuing in bulb, never in tulip; seed issuing in seed, never in bread. The Political Economy of Europe has hitherto devoted itself wholly to the multiplication, or (less even) the aggregation, of bulbs. It never saw nor conceived such a thing as a tulip. Nay, boiled bulbs they might have been—glass bulbs—Prince Rupert's drops, consummated in powder (well, if it were glass-powder and not gunpowder), for any end or meaning the economists had in defining the laws of aggregation. We will try and get a clearer notion of them.

The best and simplest general type of capital is a well-made plowshare. Now, if that plowshare did nothing but beget other plowshares, in a polypous manner,—however the great cluster of polypous plow might glitter in the sun, it would have lost its function of capital. It becomes true capital only by another kind of splendor,—when it is seen, "splendescere sulco," to grow bright in the furrow; rather with diminution of its substance, than addition, by the noble friction. And the true home question, to every capitalist and to every nation, is not, "how many plows have you?"—but, "where are your furrows?" not—"how quickly will this capital reproduce itself?"—but, "what will it do during reproduction?" What substance will it furnish, good for life? what work construct, protective of life? if none, its own reproduction is useless—if worse than none,—(for capital may destroy life as well as support it), its own reproduction is worse than useless; it is merely an advance from Tisiphone, on mortgage—not a profit by any means.

Not a profit, as the ancients truly saw, and showed in the type of Ixion; for capital is the head, or fountain head, of wealth—the "well-head" of wealth, as the clouds are the well-heads of rain: but when clouds are without water, and only beget clouds, they issue in wrath at last, instead of rain, and in lightning instead of harvest; whence Ixion is said first to have invited his guests to a banquet, and then made them fall into a pit filled with fire; which is the type of the temptation of riches issuing in imprisoned torment, —torment in a pit, (as also Demas's silver mine), after which, to show the rage of riches passing from lust of pleasure to lust of power, yet power not truly understood, Ixion is said to have desired Juno, and instead, embracing a cloud (or phantasm), to have begotten the Centaurs; the power of mere wealth being, in itself, as the embrace of a shadow,—comfortless (so also "Ephraim feedeth on wind and followeth after the east wind;" or "that which is not" —Prov. xxiii. 5; and again Dante's Geryon, the type of avaricious fraud, as he flies, gathers the *air* up with retractile claws,—"l'aer a se raccolse,"*) but in its offspring, a mingling of the brutal with the human nature: human in sagacity—using both intellect and arrow; but brutal in its body and hoof, for consuming and trampling down. For which sin Ixion is at last bound upon a wheel

---

* So also in the vision of the woman bearing the ephah, before quoted, "the wind was in their wings," not wings "of a stork," as in our version; but "*milvi*," of a kite, in the Vulgate, or perhaps more accurately still in the Septuagint, "hoopoe," a bird connected typically with the power of riches by many traditions, of which that of its petition for a crest of gold is perhaps the most interesting. The "Birds" of Aristophanes, in which its part is principal, is full of them; note especially the "fortification of the air with baked bricks, like Babylon," 1. 550; and, again, compare the Plutus of Dante, who (to show the influence of riches in destroying the reason) is the only one of the powers of the Inferno who cannot speak intelligibly; and also the cowardliest; he is not merely quelled or restrained, but literally "collapses" at a word; the sudden and helpless operation of mercantile panic being all told in the brief metaphor, "as the sails, swollen with the wind, fall, when the mast breaks."

—fiery and toothed, and rolling perpetually in the air;— the type of human labor when selfish and fruitless (kept far into the middle ages in their wheel of fortune); the wheel which has in it no breath or spirit, but is whirled by chance only; whereas of all true work the Ezekiel vision is true, that the spirit of the living creature is in the wheels, and where the angels go, the wheels go by them; but move no otherwise.

This being the real nature of capital, it follows that there are two kinds of true production, always going on in an active State; one of seed, and one of food, or production for the Ground and for the Mouth; both of which are by covetous persons thought to be production only for the granary; whereas the function of the granary is but intermediate and conservative, fulfilled in distribution; else it ends in nothing but mildew, and nourishment of rats and worms. And since production for the Ground is only useful with future hope of harvest, all *essential* production is for the Mouth; and is finally measured by the mouth; hence, as I said above, consumption is the crown of production; and the wealth of a nation is only to be estimated by what it consumes.

The want of any clear sight of this fact is the capital error, issuing in rich interest and revenue of error, among the political economists. Their minds are continually set on money-gain, not on mouth gain; and they fall into every sort of net and snare, dazzled by the coin-glitter as birds by the fowler's glass; or rather (for there is not much else like birds in them) they are like children trying to jump on the heads of their own shadows; the money-gain being only the shadow of the true gain, which is humanity.

The final object of political economy, therefore, is to get good method of consumption, and great quantity of consumption; in other words, to use everything, and to use it nobly; whether it be substance, service, or service perfecting substance. The most curious error in Mr. Mill's entire work (provided for him originally by Ricardo), is his endeavor to distinguish between direct and indirect service, and consequent assertion that a demand for commodities is not demand for labor (I. v. 9, *et seq.*). He distinguishes between laborers employed to lay out pleasure grounds, and to manufacture velvet; declaring that it makes material difference to the laboring classes in which of these two ways a capitalist spends his money; because the employment of the gardeners is a demand for labor, but the purchase of velvet is not.* Error colossal as well as strange. It will, indeed, make a difference to the laborer whether he bid him swing his scythe in the spring winds, or drive the loom in pestilential air; but, so far as his pocket is concerned, it makes to him absolutely no difference whether we order him to make green velvet, with seed and a scythe, or red velvet, with silk and scissors. Neither does it anywise concern him whether, when the velvet is made, we consume

---

* The value of raw material, which has, indeed, to be deducted from the price of the labor, is not contemplated in the passages referred to, Mr. Mill having fallen into the mistake solely by pursuing the collateral results of the payment of wages to middlemen. He says—"The consumer does not, with his own funds, pay the weaver for his day's work." Pardon me; the consumer of the velvet pays the weaver with his own funds as much as he pays the gardener. He pays, probably, an intermediate shipowner, velvet-merchant, and shopman; pays carriage money, shop rent, damage money, time money, and care money; all these are above and beside the velvet price (just as the wages of a head gardener would be above the grass price); but the velvet is as much produced by the consumer's capital, though he does not pay for it till six months after production, as the grass is produced by his capital, though he does not pay the man who mowed and rolled it on Monday, till Saturday afternoon. I do not know if Mr. Mill's conclusion,—"the capital cannot be dispensed with, the purchasers can" (p. 98), has yet been reduced to practice in the City on any large scale.

it by walking on it, or wearing it, so long as our consumption of it is wholly selfish. But if our consumption is to be in anywise unselfish, not only our mode of consuming the articles we require interests him, but also the *kind* of article we require with a view to consumption. As thus (returning for a moment to Mr. Mill's great hardware theory*): it matters, so far as the laborer's immediate profit is concerned, not an iron filing whether I employ him in growing a peach, or forging a bombshell; but my probable mode of consumption of those articles matters seriously. Admit that it is to be in both cases "unselfish," and the difference, to him, is final, whether when his child is ill, I walk into his cottage and give it the peach, or drop the shell down his chimney, and blow his roof off.

The worst of it, for the peasant, is, that the capitalist's consumption of the peach is apt to be selfish, and of the shell, distributive;† but, in all cases, that is the broad and

---

*Which, observe, is the precise opposite of the one under examination. The hardware theory required us to discharge our gardeners and engage manufacturers; the velvet theory requires us to discharge our manufacturers and engage gardeners.

† It is one very awful form of the operation of wealth in Europe that it is entirely capitalists' wealth which supports unjust wars. Just wars do not need so much money to support them; for most of the men who wage such, wage them gratis; but for an unjust war, men's bodies and souls have both to be bought; and the best tools of war for them besides; which makes such war costly to the maximum; not to speak of the cost of base fear, and angry suspicion, between nations which have not grace nor honesty enough in all their multitudes to buy an hour's peace of mind with: as, at present, France and England, purchasing of each other ten millions sterling worth of consternation annually, (a remarkably light crop, half thorns and half aspen leaves,—sown, reaped, and granaried by the "science" of the modern political economist, teaching covetousness instead of truth.) And all unjust war being supportable, if not by pillage of the enemy, only by loans from capitalists, these loans are repaid by subsequent taxation of the people, who appear to have no will in the matter, the capitalists' will being the primary root of the war; but its real root is the covetousness of the whole nation, rendering it incapable of faith, frankness, or justice, and bringing about, therefore, in due time, his own separate loss and punishment to each person.

general fact, that on due catallactic commercial principles, *somebody's* roof must go off in fulfillment of the bomb's destiny. You may grow for your neighbor, at your liking, grapes or grapeshot; he will also, catallactically, grow grapes or grapeshot for you, and you will each reap what you have sown.

It is, therefore, the manner and issue of consumption which are the real tests of production. Production does not consist in things laboriously made, but in things serviceably consumable; and the question for the nation is not how much labor it employs, but how much life it produces. For as consumption is the end and aim of production, so life is the end and aim of consumption.

I left this question to the reader's thought two months ago, choosing rather that he should work it out for himself than have it sharply stated to him. But now, the ground being sufficiently broken (and the details into which the several questions, here opened, must lead us, being too complex for discussion in the pages of a periodical, so that I must pursue them elsewhere), I desire, in closing the series of introductory papers, to leave this one great fact clearly stated. THERE IS NO WEALTH BUT LIFE. Life, including all its powers of love, of joy, and of admiration. That country is the richest which nourishes the greatest number of noble and happy human beings; that man is richest who, having perfected the functions of his own life to the utmost, has also the widest helpful influence, both personal, and by means of his possessions, over the lives of others.

A strange political economy; the only one, nevertheless, that ever was or can be: all political economy founded on self-interest* being but the fulfillment of that which once

---

* "In all reasoning about prices, the proviso must be understood, 'supposing all parties to take care of their own interest.' "— Mill, III. i. 5.

brought schism into the Policy of angels, and ruin into the Economy of Heaven.

"The greatest number of human beings noble and happy." But is the nobleness consistent with the number? Yes, not only consistent with it, but essential to it. The maximum of life can only be reached by the maximum of virtue. In this respect the law of human population differs wholly from that of animal life. The multiplication of animals is checked only by want of food, and by the hostility of races; the population of the gnat is restrained by the hunger of the swallow, and that of the swallow by the scarcity of gnats. Man, considered as an animal, is indeed limited by the same laws; hunger, or plague, or war, are the necessary and only restraints upon his increase,—effectual restraints hitherto,—his principal study having been how most swiftly to destroy himself, or ravage his dwelling-places, and his highest skill directed to give range to the famine, seed to the plague, and sway to the sword. But, considered as other than an animal, his increase is not limited by these laws. It is limited only by the limits of his courage and his love. Both of these *have* their bounds; and ought to have: his race has its bounds also; but these have not yet been reached, nor will be reached for ages.

In all the ranges of human thought I know none so melancholy as the speculations of political economists on the population question. It is proposed to better the condition of the laborer by giving him higher wages. "Nay," says the economist, "if you raise his wages, he will either people down to the same point of misery at which you found him, or drink your wages away." He will. I know it. Who gave him this will? Suppose it were your own son of whom you spoke, declaring to me that you dared not take him into your firm, nor even give him his just laborer's wages, because if you did, he would die of drunkenness, and leave half a score of children to the parish. "Who gave your son these dispositions?"—I should inquire. Has he them by inheritance or by education? By one or other they *must* come; and as in him, so also in the poor. Either these poor are of a race essentially different from ours, and unredeemable (which, however often implied, I have heard none yet openly say), or else by such care as we have ourselves received, we may make them continent and sober as ourselves—wise and dispassionate as we are—models arduous of imitation. "But," it is answered, "they cannot receive education." Why not? That is precisely the point at issue. Charitable persons suppose the worst fault of the rich is to refuse the people meat; and the people cry for their meat, kept back by fraud, to the Lord of Multitudes.* Alas! it is not meat

---

*James v. 4. Observe, in these statements I am not taking up, nor countenancing one whit, the common socialist idea of division of property; division of property is its destruction; and with it the destruction of all hope, all industry, and all justice: it is simply chaos—a chaos toward which the believers in modern political economy are fast tending, and from which I am striving to save them. The rich man does not keep back meat from the poor by retaining his riches; but by basely using them. Riches are a form of strength; and a strong man does not injure others by keeping his strength, but by using it injuriously. The socialist, seeing a strong man oppress a weak one, cries out—"Break the strong man's arms;" but I say, "Teach him to use them to better purpose." The fortitude and intelligence which acquire riches are intended, by the Giver of both, not to scatter, nor to give away, but to employ those riches in the service of mankind; in other words, in the redemption of the erring and aid of the weak—that is to say, there is first to be the work to gain money; then the Sabbath of use for it—the Sabbath, whose law is, not to lose life, but to save. It is continually the fault or the folly of the poor that they are poor, as it is usually a child's fault if it falls into a pond, and a cripple's weakness that slips at a crossing; nevertheless, most passers by would pull the child out, or help up the cripple. Put it at the worst, that all the poor of the world are but disobedient children, or careless cripples, and that all rich people are wise and strong, and you will see at once that neither is the socialist right in desiring to make everybody poor, powerless, and foolish as he is himself, nor the rich man right in leaving the children in the mire.

of which the refusal is cruelest, or to which the claim is validest. The life is more than the meat. The rich not only refuse food to the poor; they refuse wisdom; they refuse virtue; they refuse salvation. Ye sheep without shepherd, it is not the pasture that has been shut from you, but the presence. Meat! perhaps your right to that may be pleadable; but other rights have to be pleaded first. Claim your crumbs from the table, if you will; but claim them as children, not as dogs; claim your right to be fed, but claim more loudly your right to be holy, perfect, and pure.

Strange words to be used of working people: "What! holy; without any long robes nor anointing oils; these rough-jacketed, rough-worded persons; set to nameless and dishonored service? Perfect!—these, with dim eyes and cramped limbs, and slowly wakening minds? Pure—these, with sensual desire and groveling thought; foul of body, and coarse of soul?" It may be so; nevertheless, such as they are, they are the holiest, perfectest, purest persons the earth can at present show. They may be what you have said; but if so, they yet are holier than we, who have left them thus.

But what can be done for them? Who can clothe—who teach—who restrain their multitudes? What end can there be for them at last, but to consume one another?

I hope for another end, though not, indeed, from any of the three remedies for over-population commonly suggested by economists.

These three are, in brief—Colonization; Bringing in of waste lands; or Discouragement of Marriage.

The first and second of these expedients merely evade or delay the question. It will, indeed, be long before the world has been all colonized, and its deserts all brought under cultivation. But the radical question is not how much habitable land is in the world, but how many human beings ought to be maintained on a given space of habitable land.

Observe, I say, *ought* to be, not how many *can* be. Ricardo, with his usual inaccuracy, defines what he calls the "natural rate of wages" as "that which will maintain the laborer." Maintain him! yes; but how?—the question was instantly thus asked of me by a working girl, to whom I read the passage. I will amplify her question for her. "Maintain him, how?" As first, to what length of life? Out of a given number of fed persons how many are to be old—how many young; that is to say, will you arrange their maintenance so as to kill them early—say at thirty or thirty-five on the average, including deaths of weakly or ill-fed children?—or so as to enable them to live out a natural life? You will feed a greater number, in the first case,* by rapidity of succession; probably a happier number in the second: which does Mr. Ricardo mean to be their natural state, and to which state belongs the natural rate of wages?

Again: A piece of land which will only support ten idle, ignorant, and improvident persons, will support thirty or forty intelligent and industrious ones. Which of these is their natural state, and to which of them belongs the natural rate of wages?

Again: If a piece of land support forty persons in industrious ignorance; and if, tired of this ignorance, they set apart ten of their number to study the properties of cones, and the sizes of stars; the labor of these ten, being withdrawn from the ground, must either tend to the increase

---

* The quantity of life is the same in both cases; but it is differently allotted.

of food in some transitional manner, or the persons set apart for siderial and conic purposes must starve, or some one else starve instead of them. What is, therefore, the rate natural of wages of the scientific persons, and how does this relate to, or measure, their reverted or transitional productiveness?

Again: If the ground maintains, at first, forty laborers in a peaceable and pious state of mind, but they become in a few years so quarrelsome and impious that they have to set apart five, to meditate upon and settle their disputes;—ten, armed to the teeth with costly instruments, to enforce the decisions; and five to remind everybody in an eloquent manner of the existence of a God;—what will be the result upon the general power of production, and what is the "natural rate of wages" of the meditative, muscular, and oracular laborers?

Leaving these questions to be discussed, or waived, at their pleasure, by Mr. Ricardo's followers, I proceed to state the main facts bearing on that probable future of the laboring classes which has been partially glanced at by Mr. Mill. That chapter and the preceding one differ from the common writing of political economists in admitting some value in the aspect of nature, and expressing regret at the probability of the destruction of natural scenery. But we may spare our anxieties on this head. Men can neither drink steam, nor eat stone. The maximum of population on a given space of land implies also the relative maximum of edible vegetable, whether for men or cattle; it implies a maximum of pure air; and of pure water. Therefore: a maximum of wood, to transmute the air, and of sloping ground, protected by herbage from the extreme heat of the sun, to feed the streams. All England may, if it so chooses, become one manufacturing town; and Englishmen, sacrificing themselves to the good of general humanity, may live diminished lives in the midst of noise, of darkness, and of deadly exhalation. But the world cannot become a factory, nor a mine. No amount of ingenuity will ever make iron digestible by the million, nor substitute hydrogen for wine. Neither the avarice nor the rage of men will ever feed them, and however the apple of Sodom and the grape of Gomorrah may spread their table for a time with dainties of ashes, and nectar of asps—so long as men live by bread, the far away valleys must laugh as they are covered with the gold of God, and the shouts of His happy multitudes ring round the wine-press and the well.

Nor need our more sentimental economists fear the too wide spread of the formalities of a mechanical agriculture. The presence of a wise population implies the search for felicity as well as for food; nor can any population reach its maximum but through that wisdom which "rejoices" in the habitable parts of the earth. The desert has its appointed place and work; the eternal engine, whose beam is the earth's axle, whose beat is its year, and whose breath is its ocean, will still divide imperiously to their desert kingdoms, bound with unfurrowable rock, and swept by unarrested sand, their powers of frost and fire: but the zones and lands between, habitable, will be loveliest in habitation. The desire of the heart is also the light of the eyes. No scene is continually and untiringly loved, but one rich by joyful human labor; smooth in field; fair in garden; full in orchard; trim, sweet, and frequent in homestead; ringing with voices of vivid existence. No air is sweet that is silent; it is only sweet when full of low currents of under sound—triplets of birds, and murmur and chirp of insects, and deep-toned words of men, and wayward trebles of childhood. As the art of life is learned, it will

be found at last that all lovely things are also necessary:—
the wild flower by the wayside, as well as the tended corn;
and the wild birds and creatures of the forest, as well as the
tended cattle; because man doth not live by bread only,
but also by the desert manna; by every wondrous word
and unknowable work of God. Happy, in that he knew
them not, nor did his fathers know; and that round about
him reaches yet into the infinite, the amazement of his
existence.

Note, finally, that all effectual advancement toward this
true felicity of the human race must be by individual, not
public effort. Certain general measures may aid, certain
revised laws guide, such advancement; but the measure
and law which have first to be determined are those of
each man's home. We continually hear it recommended
by sagacious people to complaining neighbors (usually less
well placed in the world than themselves), that they should
"remain content in the station in which Providence has
placed them." There are perhaps some circumstances of
life in which Providence has no intention that people *should*
be content. Nevertheless, the maxim is on the whole a
good one; but it is peculiarly for home use. That your
neighbor should, or should not, remain content with *his*
position, is not your business; but it is very much your
business to remain content with your own. What is chiefly
needed in England at the present day is to show the quantity of pleasure that may be obtained by a consistent, well-administered competence, modest, confessed, and laborious.
We need examples of people who, leaving Heaven to decide
whether they are to rise in the world, decide for themselves
that they will be happy in it, and have resolved to seek—
not greater wealth, but simpler pleasure; not higher fortune,
but deeper felicity; making the first of possessions, self-

possession; and honoring themselves in the harmless pride and calm pursuits of peace.

Of which lowly peace it is written that "justice and peace have kissed each other;" and that the fruit of justice is "sown in peace of them that make peace;" not "peacemakers" in the common understanding—reconcilers of quarrels; (though that function also follows on the greater one;) but peace-Creators; Givers of Calm. Which you cannot give, unless you first gain; nor is this gain one which will follow assuredly on any course of business, commonly so called. No form of gain is less probable, business being (as is shown in the language of all nations— πωλεῖν from πέλω, πρᾶσις from περάω, venire, vendre, and venal, from venio, &c.) essentially restless—and probably contentious;—having a raven-like mind to the motion to and fro, as to the carrion food; whereas the olive-feeding and bearing birds look for rest for their feet: thus it is said of Wisdom that she "hath builded her house, and hewn out her seven pillars;" and even when, though apt to wait long at the doorposts, she has to leave her house and go abroad, her paths are peace also.

For us, at all events, her work must begin at the entry of the doors: all true economy is "Law of the house." Strive to make that law strict, simple, generous: waste nothing, and grudge nothing. Care in nowise to make more of money, but care to make much of it; remembering always the great, palpable, inevitable fact—the rule and root of all economy—that what one person has, another cannot have; and that every atom of substance, of whatever kind, used or consumed, is so much human life spent; which, if it issue in the saving present life, or gaining more, is well spent, but if not, is either so much life prevented, or so much slain. In all buying, consider, first, what condition of existence you cause in the producers of what you buy; secondly, whether the sum you have paid is just to the producer, and in due proportion, lodged in his hands;* thirdly, to how much clear use, for food, knowledge, or joy, this that you have bought can be put; and fourthly, to whom and in what way it can be most speedily and serviceably distributed: in all dealings whatsoever insisting on entire openness and stern fulfillment; and in all doings, on perfection and loveliness of accomplishment; especially on fineness and purity of all marketable commodity: watching at the same time for all ways of gaining, or teaching, powers of simple pleasure; and of showing "ὅσον ἐν ἀσφοδέλῳ γέγ' ὄνειαρ"—the sum of enjoyment depending not on the quantity of things tasted, but on the vivacity and patience of taste.

And if, on due and honest thought over these things, it seems that the kind of existence to which men are now summoned by every plea of pity and claim of right, may, for some time at least, not to be a luxurious one;—consider whether, even supposing it guiltless, luxury would be desired by any of us, if we saw clearly at our sides the suffering which accompanies it in the world. Luxury is indeed possible in the future—innocent and exquisite; luxury for all, and by the help of all: but luxury at present can only be enjoyed by the ignorant; the cruelest man living could not sit at his feast, unless he sat blindfold.

---

*The proper offices of middle-men, namely, overseers (or authoritative workmen), conveyancers (merchants, sailors, retail dealers, &c.), and ordertakers (persons employed to receive directions from the consumer), must, of course, be examined before I can enter further into the question of just payment of the first producer. But I have not spoken of them in these introductory papers, because the evils attendant on the abuse of such intermediate functions result not from any alleged principle of modern political economy, but from private carelessness or iniquity.

Raise the veil boldly; face the light; and if, as yet, the light of the eye can only be through tears, and the light of the body through sackcloth, go thou forth weeping, bearing precious seed, until the time come, and the kingdom, when Christ's gift of bread and bequest of peace shall be Unto this last as unto thee; and when, for earth's severed multitudes of the wicked and the weary, there shall be holier reconciliation than that of the narrow home, and calm economy, where the Wicked cease—not from trouble, but from troubling—and the Weary are at rest.

BOOK II.

TWO LECTURES ON WORK AND TRAFFIC

FROM

"THE CROWN OF WILD OLIVE."

PREFACE

TWENTY YEARS ago, there was no lovelier piece of lowland scenery in South England, nor any more pathetic in the world, by its expression of sweet human character and life, than that immediately bordering on the sources of the Wandle, and including the lower moors of Addington, and the villages of Beddington and Carshalton, with all their pools and streams. No clearer or diviner waters ever sang with constant lips of the hand which "giveth rain from heaven;" no pastures ever lightened in spring time with more passionate blossoming; no sweeter homes ever hallowed the heart of the passer-by with their pride of peaceful gladness—fain-hidden—yet full-confessed. The place remains, or, until a few months ago, remained, nearly unchanged in its larger features; but, with deliberate mind I say, that I have never seen anything so ghastly in its inner tragic meaning,—not in Pisan Maremma—not by Campagna tomb,—not by the sand-isles of the Torcellan shore,—as the slow stealing of aspects of reckless, indolent, animal neglect, over the delicate sweetness of that English scene: nor is any blasphemy or impiety—any frantic saying or godless thought—more appalling to me, using the best power of judgment I have to discern its sense and scope, than the insolent defilings of those springs by the human herds that drink of them. Just where the welling of stainless water, trembling and pure, like a body of light, enters the pool of Carshalton, cutting itself a radiant channel down to the gravel, through warp of feathery weeds, all waving, which it traverses with its deep threads of clearness, like the chalcedony in moss-agate, starred here and there with white grenouillette; just in the very rush and murmur of the first spreading currents, the human wretches of the place cast their street and house foulness; heaps of dust and slime, and broken shreds of old metal, and rags of putrid clothes; they having neither energy to cart it away, nor decency enough to dig it into the ground, thus shed into the stream, to diffuse what venom of it will float and melt, far away, in all places where God meant those waters to bring joy and health. And, in a little pool, behind some houses further in the village, where another spring rises, the shattered stones of the well, and of the little fretted channel which was long ago built and traced for it by gentler hands, lie scattered, each from each, under a ragged bank of mortar, and scoria, and bricklayers' refuse, on one side, which the clean water nevertheless chastises to purity; but it cannot conquer the dead earth beyond; and there, circled and coiled under festering scum, the stagnant edge of the pool effaces itself into a slope of black slime, the accumulation of indolent years. Half-a-dozen men, with one day's work, could cleanse those pools, and trim the flowers about their banks, and make every breath of summer air above them rich with cool balm; and every glittering wave medicinal, as if it ran, troubled of angels, from the porch of Bethesda. But that day's work is never given, nor will be; nor will any joy be possible to heart of man, for evermore, about those wells of English waters.

When I last left them, I walked up slowly through the back streets of Croydon, from the old church to the hospital; and, just on the left, before coming up to the crossing of the High Street, there was a new public-house built. And the front of it was built in so wise manner, that a recess of two feet was left below its front windows, between them and the street-pavement—a recess too narrow for any possible use (for even if it had been occupied by a seat, as in old time it might have been, everybody walking along the street would have fallen over the legs of the reposing wayfarers). But, by way of making this two feet depth of freehold land more expressive of the dignity of an establishment for the sale of spirituous liquors, it was fenced from the pavement by an imposing iron railing, having four or five spearheads to the yard of it, and six feet high; containing as much iron and iron-work, indeed, as could well be put into the space; and by this stately arrangement, the little piece of dead ground within, between wall and street, became a protective receptacle of refuse; cigar ends, and oyster shells, and the like, such as an open-handed English street-populace habitually scatters from its presence, and was thus left, unsweepable by any ordinary methods. Now the iron bars which, uselessly (or in great degree worse than uselessly), enclosed this bit of ground, and made it pestilent, represented a quantity of work which would have cleansed the Carshalton pools three times over;—of work, partly cramped and deadly, in the mine; partly fierce* and

---

* "A fearful occurrence took place a few days since, near Wolverhampton. Thomas Snape, aged nineteen, was on duty as the 'keeper' of a blast furnace at Deepfield, assisted by John Gardner, aged eighteen, and Joseph Swift, aged thirty-seven. The furnace contained four tons of molten iron, and an equal amount of cinders, and ought to have been run out at 7.30 P.M. But Snape and his mates, engaged in talking and drinking, neglected their duty, and in the meantime, the iron rose in the furnace until it reached a pipe wherein water was contained. Just as the men had stripped, and were proceeding to tap the furnace, the water in the pipe, converted into steam, burst down its front and let loose on them the molten metal, which instantaneously consumed Gardner;

exhaustive, at the furnace; partly foolish and sedentary, of ill-taught students making bad designs: work from the beginning to the last fruits of it, and in all the branches of it, venomous, deathful, and miserable. Now, how did it come to pass that this work was done instead of the other; that the strength and life of the English operative were spent in defiling ground, instead of redeeming it; and in producing an entirely (in that place) valueless piece of metal, which can neither be eaten nor breathed, instead of medicinal fresh air, and pure water?

There is but one reason for it, and at present a conclusive one,—that the capitalist can charge percentage on the work in the one case, and cannot in the other. If, having certain funds for supporting labor at my disposal, I pay men merely to keep my ground in order, my money is, in that function, spent once for all; but if I pay them to dig iron out of my ground, and work it, and sell it, I can charge rent for the ground, and percentage both on the manufacture and the sale, and make my capital profitable in these three bye-ways. The greater part of the profitable investment of capital, in the present day, is in operations of this kind, in which the public is persuaded to buy something of no use to it, on production, or sale, of which, the capitalist may charge percentage; the said public remaining all the while under the persuasion that the percentages thus obtained are real national gains, whereas, they are merely filchings out of partially light pockets, to swell heavy ones.

Snape, terribly burnt, and mad with pain, leaped into the canal and then ran home and fell dead on the threshold, Swift survived to reach the hospital, where he died too."

In further illustration of this matter, I beg the reader to look at the article on the "Decay of the English Race," in the *Pall-Mall Gazette* of April 17, of this year; and at the articles on the "Report of the Thames Commission," in any journals of the same date.

Thus, the Croydon publican buys the iron railing, to make himself more conspicuous to drunkards. The public-housekeeper on the other side of the way presently buys another railing, to out-rail him with. Both are, as to their *relative* attractiveness to customers of taste, just where they were before; but they have lost the price of the railings; which they must either themselves finally lose, or make their aforesaid customers of taste pay, by raising the price of their beer, or adulterating it. Either the publicans, or their customers, are thus poorer by precisely what the capitalist has gained; and the value of the work itself, meantime, has been lost to the nation; the iron bars in that form and place being wholly useless. It is this mode of taxation of the poor by the rich which is referred to in the text (page 136), in comparing the modern acquisitive power of capital with that of the lance and sword; the only difference being that the levy of black-mail in old times was by force, and is now by cozening. The old rider and reiver frankly quartered himself on the publican for the night; the modern one merely makes his lance into an iron spike, and persuades his host to buy it. One comes as an open robber, the other as a cheating pedlar; but the result, to the injured person's pocket, is absolutely the same. Of course many useful industries mingle with, and disguise the useless ones; and in the habits of energy aroused by the struggle, there is a certain direct good. It is far better to spend four thousand pounds in making a good gun, and then to blow it to pieces, than to pass life in idleness. Only do not let it be called "political economy." There is also a confused notion in the minds of many persons, that the gathering of the property of the poor into the hands of the rich does no ultimate harm; since, in whosesoever hands it may be, it must be spent at last, and thus, they think, return to the poor again. This fallacy has been again and again exposed; but grant the plea true, and the same apology may, of course, be made for black-mail, or any other form of robbery. It might be (though practically it never is) as advantageous for the nation that the robber should have the spending of the money he extorts, as that the person robbed should have spent it. But this is no excuse for the theft. If I were to put a turnpike on the road where it passes my own gate, and endeavor to exact a shilling from every passenger, the public would soon do away with my gate, without listening to any plea on my part that "it was as advantageous to them, in the end, that I should spend their shillings, as that they themselves should." But if, instead of out-facing them with a turnpike, I can only persuade them to come in and buy stones, or old iron, or any other useless thing, out of my ground, I may rob them to the same extent, and be, moreover, thanked as a public benefactor, and promoter of commercial prosperity. And this main question for the poor of England— for the poor of all countries—is wholly omitted in every common treatise on the subject of wealth. Even by the laborers themselves, the operation of capital is regarded only in its effect on their immediate interests; never in the far more terrific power of its appointment of the kind and the object of labor. It matters little, ultimately, how much a laborer is paid for making anything; but it matters fearfully what the thing is, which he is compelled to make. If his labor is so ordered as to produce food, and fresh air, and fresh water, no matter that his wages are low;—the food and fresh air and water will be at last there; and he will at last get them. But if he is paid to destroy food and fresh air, or to produce iron bars instead of them,—the food and air will finally *not* be there, and he will *not* get them, to his great and final inconvenience. So that, conclusively, in political as in household economy, the great question is, not so much what money you have in your pocket, as what you will buy with it, and do with it.

I have been long accustomed, as all men engaged in work of investigation must be, to hear my statements laughed at for years, before they are examined or believed; and I am generally content to wait the public's time. But it has not been without displeased surprise that I have found myself totally unable, as yet, by any repetition, or illustration, to force this plain thought into my readers' heads,—that the wealth of nations, as of men, consists in substance, not in ciphers; and that the real good of all work, and of all commerce, depends on the final worth of the thing you make, or get by it. This is a practical enough statement, one would think: but the English public has been so possessed by its modern school of economists with the notion that Business is always good, whether it be busy in mischief or in benefit; and that buying and selling are always salutary, whatever the intrinsic worth of what you buy or sell,—that it seems impossible to gain so much as a patient hearing for any inquiry respecting the substantial result of our eager modern labors. I have never felt more checked by the sense of this impossibility than in arranging the heads of the following three lectures,* which, though delivered at considerable intervals of time, and in different places, were not prepared without reference to each other. Their connection would, however, have been made far more distinct, if I had not been prevented, by what I feel to be another great difficulty in addressing

---

*The Third Lecture in *The Crown of Wild Olive*, on War, we do not print from lack of space as not bearing directly upon the subject of this collection.—Ed.

English audiences, from enforcing, with any decision, the common, and to me the most important, part of their subjects. I chiefly desired (as I have just said) to question my hearers—operatives, merchants, and soldiers, as to the ultimate meaning of the *business* they had in hand; and to know from them what they expected or intended their manufacture to come to, their selling to come to, and their killing to come to. That appeared the first point needing determination before I could speak to them with any real utility or effect. "You craftsmen—salesmen—swordsmen,— do but tell me clearly what you want, then, if I can say anything to help you, I will; and if not, I will account to you as I best may for my inability." But in order to put this question into any terms, one had first of all to face the difficulty just spoken of—to me for the present insuperable, —the difficulty of knowing whether to address one's audience as believing, or not believing, in any other world than this. For if you address any average modern English company as believing in an Eternal life, and endeavor to draw any conclusions, from this assumed belief, as to their present business, they will forthwith tell you that what you say is very beautiful, but it is not practical. If, on the contrary, you frankly address them as unbelievers in Eternal life, and try to draw any consequences from that unbelief,— they immediately hold you for an accursed person, and shake off the dust from their feet at you. And the more I thought over what I had got to say, the less I found I could say it, without some reference to this intangible or intractable part of the subject. It made all the difference, in asserting any principle of war, whether one assumed that a discharge of artillery would merely knead down a certain quantity of red clay into a level line, as in a brick field; or whether, out of every separately Christian-named portion of the ruinous heap, there went out, into the smoke and dead-fallen air of battle, some astonished condition of soul, unwillingly released. It made all the difference, in speaking of the possible range of commerce, whether one assumed that all bargains related only to visible property—or whether property, for the present invisible, but nevertheless real, was elsewhere purchasable on other terms. It made all the difference, in addressing a body of men subject to considerable hardship, and having to find some way out of it—whether one could confidentially say to them, "My friends,—you have only to die, and all will be right;" or whether one had any secret misgiving that such advice was more blessed to him that gave, than to him that took it. And therefore the deliberate reader will find, throughout these lectures, a hesitation in driving points home, and a pausing short of conclusions which he will feel I would fain have come to; hesitation which arises wholly from this uncertainty of my hearers' temper. For I do not now speak, nor have I ever spoken, since the time of my first forward youth, in any proselyting temper, as desiring to persuade any one of what, in such matters, I thought myself; but, whomsoever I venture to address, I take for the time his creed as I find it; and endeavor to push it into such vital fruit as it seems capable of. Thus, it is a creed with a great part of the existing English people, that they are in possession of a book which tells them, straight from the lips of God, all they ought to do, and need to know. I have read that book, with as much care as most of them, for some forty years; and am thankful that, on those who trust it, I can press its pleadings. My endeavor has been uniformly to make them trust it more deeply than they do; trust it, not in their own favorite verses only, but in the sum of all; trust it not as a fetich or talisman, which they are to be saved by daily repetitions of; but as a Captain's order, to be heard and obeyed at their peril. I was always encouraged by supposing my hearers to hold such belief. To these, if to any, I once had hope of addressing, with acceptance, words which insisted on the guilt of pride, and the futility of avarice; from these, if from any, I once expected ratification of a political economy, which asserted that the life was more than the meat, and the body than raiment; and these, it once seemed to me, I might ask without accusation of fanaticism, not merely in doctrine of the lips, but in the bestowal of their heart's treasure, to separate themselves from the crowd of whom it is written, "After all these things do the Gentiles seek."

It cannot, however, be assumed, with any semblance of reason, that a general audience is now wholly, or even in majority, composed of these religious persons. A large portion must always consist of men who admit no such creed; or who, at least, are inaccessible to appeals founded on it. And as, with the so-called Christian, I desired to plead for honest declaration and fulfillment of his belief in life,—with the so-called Infidel, I desired to plead for an honest declaration and fulfillment of his belief in death. The dilemma is inevitable. Men must either hereafter live, or hereafter die; fate may be bravely met, and conduct wisely ordered, on either expectation; but never in hesitation between ungrasped hope, and unconfronted fear. We usually believe in immortality, so far as to avoid preparation for death; and in mortality, so far as to avoid preparation for anything after death. Whereas, a wise man will at least hold himself prepared for one or other of two events, of which one or other is inevitable; and will have all things in order, for his sleep, or in readiness, for his awakening.

Nor have we any right to call it an ignoble judgment,

if he determine to put them in order, as for sleep. A brave belief in life is indeed an enviable state of mind, but, as far as I can discern, an unusual one. I know few Christians so convinced of the splendor of the rooms in their Father's house, as to be happier when their friends are called to those mansions, than they would have been if the Queen had sent for them to live at Court: nor has the Church's most ardent "desire to depart, and be with Christ," ever cured it of the singular habit of putting on mourning for every person summoned to such departure. On the contrary, a brave belief in death has been assuredly held by many not ignoble persons, and it is a sign of the last depravity in the Church itself, when it assumes that such a belief is inconsistent with either purity of character, or energy of hand. The shortness of life is not, to any rational person, a conclusive reason for wasting the space of it which may be granted him; nor does the anticipation of death to-morrow suggest, to any one but a drunkard, the expediency of drunkenness to-day. To teach that there is no device in the grave, may indeed make the deviceless person more contented in his dullness; but it will make the deviser only more earnest in devising, nor is human conduct likely, in every case, to be purer under the conviction that all its evil may in a moment be pardoned, and all its wrong-doing in a moment redeemed; and that the sigh of repentance, which purges the guilt of the past, will waft the soul into a felicity which forgets its pain,—than it may be under the sterner, and to many not unwise minds, more probable, apprehension, that "what a man soweth that shall he also reap"—or others reap,—when he, the living seed of pestilence, walketh no more in darkness, but lies down therein.

But to men whose feebleness of sight, or bitterness of

soul, or the offence given by the conduct of those who claim higher hope, may have rendered this painful creed the only possible one, there is an appeal to be made, more secure in its ground than any which can be addressed to happier persons. I would fain, if I might offenselessly, have spoken to them as if none others heard; and have said thus: Hear me, you dying men, who will soon be deaf forever. For these others, at your right hand and your left, who look forward to a state of infinite existence, in which all their errors will be overruled, and all their faults forgiven; for these, who, stained and blackened in the battle smoke of mortality, have but to dip themselves for an instant in the font of death, and to rise renewed of plumage, as a dove that is covered with silver, and her feathers like gold; for these, indeed, it may be permissible to waste their numbered moments, through faith in a future of innumerable hours; to these, in their weakness, it may be conceded that they should tamper with sin which can only bring forth fruit of righteousness, and profit by the iniquity which, one day, will be remembered no more. In them, it may be no sign of hardness of heart to neglect the poor, over whom they know their Master is watching; and to leave those to perish temporarily, who cannot perish eternally. But, for you, there is no such hope, and therefore no such excuse. This fate, which you ordain for the wretched, you believe to be all their inheritance; you may crush them, before the moth, and they will never rise to rebuke you;—their breath, which fails for lack of food, once expiring, will never be recalled to whisper against you a word of accusing;—they and you, as you think, shall lie down together in the dust, and the worms cover you;—and for them there shall be no consolation, and on you no vengeance,—only the question murmured above your grave:

"Who shall repay him what he hath done?" Is it therefore easier for you in your heart to inflict the sorrow for which there is no remedy? Will you take, wantonly, this little all of his life from your poor brother, and make his brief hours long to him with pain? Will you be readier to the injustice which can never be redressed; and niggardly of mercy which you *can* bestow but once, and which, refusing, you refuse forever? I think better of you, even of the most selfish, than that you would do this, well understood. And for yourselves, it seems to me, the question becomes not less grave, in these curt limits. If your life were but a fever fit,—the madness of a night, whose follies were all to be forgotten in the dawn, it might matter little how you fretted away the sickly hours,—what toys you snatched at, or let fall,—what visions you followed wistfully with the deceived eyes of sleepless phrenzy. Is the earth only an hospital? Play, if you care to play, on the floor of the hospital dens. Knit its straw into what crowns please you; gather the dust of it for treasure, and die rich in that, clutching at the black motes in the air with your dying hands;—and yet, it may be well with you. But if this life be no dream, and the world no hospital; if all the peace and power and joy you can ever win, must be won now; and all fruit of victory gathered here, or never;—will you still, throughout the puny totality of your life, weary yourselves in the fire for vanity? If there is no rest which remaineth for you, is there none you might presently take? was this grass of the earth made green for your shroud only, not for your bed? and can you never lie down *upon* it, but only *under* it? The heathen, to whose creed you have returned, thought not so. They knew that life brought its contest, but they expected from it also the crown of all contest: No proud one! no jeweled circlet flaming through Heaven above the hight of the unmerited throne; only some few leaves of wild olive, cool to the tired brow, through a few years of peace. It should have been of gold, they thought; but Jupiter was poor; this was the best the god could give them. Seeking a greater than this, they had known it a mockery. Not in war, not in wealth, not in tyranny, was there any happiness to be found for them—only in kindly peace, fruitful and free. The wreath was to be of *wild* olive, mark you:—the tree that grows carelessly, tufting the rocks with no vivid bloom, no verdure of branch; only with soft snow of blossom, and scarcely fulfilled fruit, mixed with grey leaf and thornset stem; no fastening of diadem for you but with such sharp embroidery! But this, such as it is, you may win while yet you live; type of grey honor and sweet rest.* Free-heartedness, and graciousness, and undisturbed trust, and requited love, and the sight of the peace of others, and the ministry to their pain;—these, and the blue sky above you, and the sweet waters and flowers of the earth beneath; and mysteries and presences, innumerable, of living things,—these may yet be here your riches; untormenting and divine: serviceable for the life that now is; nor, it may be, without promise of that which is to come.

---

* μελιτόεσσα, ἀέθλων γ' ἕνεκεν.

THE CROWN OF WILD OLIVE

LECTURE I.
WORK.

(Delivered before the Working Men's Institute, at Camberwell.)

MY FRIENDS,—I have not come among you to-night to endeavor to give you an entertaining lecture; but to tell you a few plain facts, and ask you some plain, but necessary questions. I have seen and known too much of the struggle for life among our laboring population, to feel at ease, even under any circumstances, in inviting them to dwell on the trivialities of my own studies; but, much more, as I meet to-night, for the first time, the members of a working Institute established in the district in which I have passed the greater part of my life, I am desirous that we should at once understand each other, on graver matters. I would fain tell you, with what feelings, and with what hope, I regard this Institution, as one of many such, now happily established throughout England, as well as in other countries;— Institutions which are preparing the way for a great change in all the circumstances of industrial life; but of which the success must wholly depend upon our clearly understanding the circumstances and necessary *limits* of this change. No teacher can truly promote the cause of education, until he knows the conditions of the life for which that education is to prepare his pupil. And the fact that he is called upon to address you nominally, as a "Working Class," must compel him, if he is in any wise earnest or thoughtful, to inquire in the outset, on what you yourselves suppose this class distinction has been founded in the past, and must be founded in the future. The manner of the amusement, and the matter of the teaching, which any of us can offer you, must depend wholly on our first understanding from you, whether you think the distinction heretofore drawn between working men and others, is truly or falsely founded. Do you accept it as it stands? do you wish it to be modified? or do you think the object of education is to efface it, and make us forget it for ever?

Let me make myself more distinctly understood. We call this—you and I—a "Working Men's" Institute, and our college in London, a "Working Men's" College. Now, how do you consider that these several institutes differ, or ought to differ, from "idle men's" institutes and "idle men's" colleges? Or by what other word than "idle" shall I distinguish those whom the happiest and wisest of working men do not object to call the "Upper Classes?" Are there really upper classes,—are there lower? How much should they always be elevated, how much always depressed? And, gentlemen and ladies—I pray those of you who are here to forgive me the offense there may be in what I am going to say. It is not *I* who wish to say it. Bitter voices say it; voices of battle and of famine through all the world, which must be heard some day, whoever keeps silence. Neither is it to *you* specially that I say it. I am sure that most now present know their duties of kindness, and fulfill them, better perhaps than I do mine. But I speak to you as representing your whole class, which errs, I know, chiefly by thoughtlessness, but not, therefore, the less terribly. Willful error is limited by the will, but what limit is there to that of which we are unconscious?

Bear with me, therefore, while I turn to these workmen, and ask them, also as representing a great multitude, what they think the "upper classes" are, and ought to be, in relation to them. Answer, you workmen who are here, as you would among yourselves, frankly; and tell me how you would have me call those classes. Am I to call them —would *you* think me right in calling them—the idle classes? I think you would feel somewhat uneasy, and as if I were not treating my subject honestly, or speaking from my heart, if I went on under the supposition that all rich people were idle. You would be both unjust and unwise if you allowed me to say that;—not less unjust than the rich people who say that all the poor are idle, and will never work if they can help it, or more than they can help.

For indeed the fact is, that there are idle poor and idle rich; and there are busy poor and busy rich. Many a beggar is as lazy as if he had ten thousand a year; and many a man of large fortune is busier than his errand-boy, and never would think of stopping in the street to play marbles. So that, in a large view, the distinction between workers and idlers, as between knaves and honest men, runs through the very heart and innermost economies of men of all ranks and in all positions. There is a working class—strong and happy—among both rich and poor; there is an idle class—weak, wicked, and miserable— among both rich and poor. And the worst of the misunderstandings arising between the two orders come of the unlucky fact that the wise of one class habitually contemplate the foolish of the other. If the busy rich people watched and rebuked the idle rich people, all would be right; and if the busy poor people watched and rebuked the idle poor people, all would be right. But each class has a tendency to look for the faults of the other. A hard-working man of property is particularly offended by an idle beggar; and an orderly, but poor, workman is naturally intolerant of the licentious luxury of the rich. And what is severe judgment in the minds of the just men of either class, becomes fierce enmity in the unjust—but among the unjust *only*. None but the dissolute among the poor look upon the rich as their natural enemies, or desire to pillage their houses and divide their property. None but the dissolute among the rich speak in opprobrious terms of the vices and follies of the poor.

There is, then, no class distinction between idle and industrious people; and I am going to-night to speak only of the industrious. The idle people we will put out of our thoughts at once—they are mere nuisances—what ought to be done with *them*, we'll talk of at another time. But there are class distinctions, among the industrious themselves; tremendous distinctions, which rise and fall to every degree in the infinite thermometer of human pain and of human power—distinctions of high and low, of lost and won, to the whole reach of man's soul and body.

These separations we will study, and the laws of them, among energetic men only, who, whether they work or whether they play, put their strength into the work, and their strength into the game; being in the full sense of the word "industrious," one way or another—with a purpose, or without. And these distinctions are mainly four:

I. Between those who work, and those who play.

II. Between those who produce the means of life, and those who consume them.

III. Between those who work with the head, and those who work with the hand.

IV. Between those who work wisely, and who work foolishly.

For easier memory, let us say we are going to oppose, in our examination.—

    I. Work to play;
    II. Production to consumption;
    III. Head to Hand; and,
    IV. Sense to nonsense.

I. First, then, of the distinction between the classes who work and the classes who play. Of course we must agree upon a definition of these terms,—work and play,—before going further. Now, roughly, not with vain subtlety of definition, but for plain use of the words, "play" is an exertion of body or mind, made to please ourselves, and with no determined end; and work is a thing done because it ought to be done, and with a determined end. You play, as you call it, at cricket, for instance. That is as hard work as anything else; but it amuses you, and it has no result but the amusement. If it were done as an ordered form of exercise, for health's sake, it would become work directly. So, in like manner, whatever we do to please ourselves, and only for the sake of the pleasure, not for an ultimate object, is "play," the "pleasing thing," not the useful thing. Play may be useful in a secondary sense (nothing is indeed more useful or necessary); but the use of it depends on its being spontaneous.

Let us, then, inquire together what sort of games the playing class in England spend their lives in playing at.

The first of all English games is making money. That is an all-absorbing game; and we knock each other down oftener in playing at that than at foot-ball, or any other roughest sport; and it is absolutely without purpose; no one who engages heartily in that game ever knows why.

Ask a great money-maker what he wants to do with his money—he never knows. He doesn't make it to do anything with it. He gets it only that he *may* get it. "What will you make of what you have got?" you ask. "Well, I'll get more," he says. Just as, at cricket, you get more runs. There's no use in the runs, but to get more of them than other people is the game. And there's no use in the money, but to have more of it than other people is the game. So all that great foul city of London there,—rattling, growling, smoking, stinking,—a ghastly heap of fermenting brickwork, pouring out poison at every pore,—you fancy it is a city of work? Not a street of it! It is a great city of play; very nasty play, and very hard play, but still play. It is only Lord's cricket ground without the turf,—a huge billiard table without the cloth, and with pockets as deep as the bottomless pit; but mainly a billiard table, after all.

Well, the first great English game is this playing at counters. It differs from the rest in that it appears always to be producing money, while every other game is expensive. But it does not always produce money. There's a great difference between "winning" money and "making" it; a great difference between getting it out of another man's pocket into ours, or filling both. Collecting money is by no means the same thing as making it; the tax-gatherer's house is not the Mint; and much of the apparent gain (so called), in commerce, is only a form of taxation on carriage or exchange.

Our next great English game, however, hunting and shooting, is costly altogether; and how much we are fined for it annually in land, horses, gamekeepers, and game laws, and all else that accompanies that beautiful and special English game, I will not endeavor to count now: but note only that, except for exercise, this is not merely a useless game, but a deadly one, to all connected with it. For through horse-racing, you get every form of what the higher classes everywhere call "Play," in distinction from all other plays; that is—gambling; by no means a beneficial or recreative game: and, through game-preserving, you get also some curious laying out of ground; that beautiful arrangement of dwelling-house for man and beast, by which we have grouse and black-cock—so many brace to the acre, and men and women—so many brace to the garret. I often wonder what the angelic builders and surveyors— the angelic builders who build the "many mansions" up above there; and the angelic surveyors, who measured that four-square city with their measuring reeds—I wonder what they think, or are supposed to think, of the laying out of ground by this nation, which has set itself, as it seems, literally to accomplish, word for word, or rather fact for word, in the persons of those poor whom its Master left to represent him, what that Master said of himself— that foxes and birds had homes, but He none.

Then, next to the gentlemen's game of hunting, we must put the ladies' game of dressing. It is not the cheapest of games. I saw a brooch at a jeweler's in Bond Street a fortnight ago, not an inch wide, and without any singular jewel in it, yet worth £3,000. And I wish I could tell you what this "play" costs, altogether, in England, France, and Russia annually. But it is a pretty game, and on certain terms, I like it; nay, I don't see it played quite as much as I would fain have it. You ladies like to lead the fashion :—by all means lead it—lead it thoroughly, lead it far enough. Dress yourselves nicely, and dress everybody else nicely. Lead the *fashions for the poor* first; make *them* look well, and you yourselves will look, in ways of which you have now no conception, all the better. The fashions you have set for some time among your peasantry are not pretty ones; their doublets are too irregularly slashed, and the wind blows too frankly through them.

Then there are other games, wild enough, as I could show you if I had time.

There's playing at literature, and playing at art—very different, both, from working at literature, or working at art, but I've no time to speak of these. I pass to the greatest of all—the play of plays, the great gentleman's game, which ladies like them best to play at,—the game of War. It is entrancingly pleasant to the imagination; the facts of it, not always so pleasant. We dress for it, however, more finely than for any other sport; and go out to it, not merely in scarlet, as to hunt, but in scarlet and gold, and all manner of fine colors: of course we could fight better in gray, and without feathers; but all nations have agreed that it is good to be well dressed at this play. Then the bats and balls are very costly; our English and French bats, with the balls and wickets, even those which we don't make any use of, costing, I suppose, now about fifteen millions of money annually to each nation; all of which, you know is paid for by hard laborer's work in the furrow and furnace. A costly game!—not to speak of its consequences; I will say at present nothing of these. The mere immediate cost of all these plays is what I want you to consider; they all cost deadly work somewhere, as many of us know too well. The jewel-cutter, whose sight fails over the diamonds; the weaver, whose arm fails over the web; the iron-forger, whose breath fails before the furnace —*they* know what work is—they, who have all the work, and none of the play, except a kind they have named for themselves down in the black north country, where "play" means being laid up by sickness. It is a pretty example for philologists, of varying dialect, this change in the sense of the word "play," as used in the black country of Birmingham, and the red and black country of Baden Baden. Yes, gentlemen, and gentlewomen, of England, who think "one moment unamused a misery, not made for feeble man," this is what you have brought the word "play" to mean, in the heart of merry England! You may have your fluting and piping; but there are sad children sitting in the marketplace, who indeed cannot say to you, "We have piped unto you, and ye have not danced;" but eternally shall say to you, "We have mourned unto you, and ye have not lamented."

This, then, is the first distinction between the "upper and lower" classes. And this is one which is by no means necessary; which indeed must, in process of good time, be by all honest men's consent abolished. Men will be taught that an existence of play, sustained by the blood of other creatures, is a good existence for gnats and sucking fish; but not for men: that neither days, nor lives, can be made holy by doing nothing in them: that the best prayer at the beginning of a day is that we may not lose its moments; and the best grace before meat, the consciousness that we have justly earned our dinner. And when we have this much of plain Christianity preached to us again, and enough respect for what we regard as inspiration, as not to think that "Son, go work to-day in my vineyard," means "Fool, go play to-day in my vineyard," we shall all be workers, in one way or another; and this much at least of the distinction between "upper" and "lower" forgotten.

II. I pass then to our second distinction; between the rich and poor, between Dives and Lazarus,—distinction which exists more sternly, I suppose, in this day, than ever in the world, Pagan or Christian, till now. I will put it sharply before you, to begin with, merely by reading two paragraphs which I cut from two papers that lay on my breakfast table on the same morning, the 25th of November, 1864. The piece about the rich Russian at Paris is common-place enough, and stupid besides (for fifteen francs, —12s. 6d.,—is nothing for a rich man to give for a couple of peaches, out of season). Still, the two paragraphs printed on the same day are worth putting side by side.

"Such a man is now here. He is a Russian, and, with your permission, we will call him Count Teufelskine. In dress he is sublime; art is considered in that toilet, the harmony of color respected, the *chiar' oscuro* evident in well-selected contrast. In manners he is dignified—nay, perhaps apathetic; nothing disturbs the placid serenity of that calm exterior. One day our friend breakfasted *chez* Bignon. When the bill came he read, 'Two peaches, 15f.' He paid. 'Peaches scarce, I presume?' was his sole remark. 'No, sir,' replied the waiter, 'but Teufelskines are.'"—*Telegraph*, November 25, 1864.

"Yesterday morning, at eight o'clock, a woman, passing a dung heap in the stone yard near the recently-erected almshouses in Shadwell Gap, High Street, Shadwell, called the attention of a Thames police-constable to a man in a sitting position on the dung heap, and said she was afraid he was dead. Her fears proved to be true. The wretched creature appeared to have been dead several hours. He had perished of cold and wet, and the rain had been beating down on him all night. The deceased was a bone-picker. He was in the lowest stage of poverty, poorly clad, and half-starved. The police had frequently driven him away from the stone yard, between sunset and sunrise, and told him to go home. He selected a most desolate spot for his wretched death. A penny and some bones were found in his pockets. The deceased was between fifty and sixty years of age. Inspector Roberts, of the K division, has given directions for inquiries to be made at the lodging-houses respecting the deceased, to ascertain his identity if possible."—*Morning Post*, November 25, 1864.

You have the separation thus in brief compass; and I want you to take notice of the "a penny and some bones were found in his pockets," and to compare it with this third statement, from the *Telegraph* of January 16th of this year :—

"Again, the dietary scale for adult and juvenile paupers was drawn up by the most conspicuous political economists in England. It is low in quantity, but it is sufficient to support nature; yet within ten years of the passing of the Poor Law Act, we heard of the paupers in the Andover Union gnawing the scraps of putrid flesh and sucking the marrow from the bones of horses which they were employed to crush."

You see my reason for thinking that our Lazarus of Christianity has some advantage over the Jewish one. Jewish Lazarus expected, or at least prayed, to be fed with crumbs from the rich man's table; but *our* Lazarus is fed with crumbs from the dog's table.

Now this distinction between rich and poor rests on two bases. Within its proper limits, on a basis which is lawful and everlastingly necessary; beyond them, on a basis unlawful, and everlastingly corrupting the frame-work of society. The lawful basis of wealth is, that a man who works should be paid the fair value of his work; and that if he does not choose to spend it to-day, he should have free leave to keep it, and spend it to-morrow. Thus, an industrious man working daily, and laying by daily, attains at last the possession of an accumulated sum of wealth, to which he has absolute right. The idle person who will not work, and the wasteful person who lays nothing by, at the end of the same time will be doubly poor—poor in possession, and dissolute in moral habit; and he will then naturally covet the money which the other has saved. And if he is then allowed to attack the other, and rob him of his well-earned wealth, there is no more any motive for saving, or any reward for good conduct; and all society is thereupon dissolved, or exists only in systems of rapine. Therefore the first necessity of social life is the clearness of national conscience in enforcing the law—that he should keep who has JUSTLY EARNED.

That law, I say, is the proper basis of distinction between rich and poor. But there is also a false basis of distinction; namely, the power held over those who earn wealth by those who levy or exact it. There will be always a number of men who would fain set themselves to the accumulation of wealth as the sole object of their lives. Necessarily, that class of men is an uneducated class, inferior in intellect, and more or less cowardly. It is physically impossible for a well-educated, intellectual, or brave man to make money the chief object of his thoughts; as physically impossible as it is for him to make his dinner the principal object of them. All healthy people like their dinners, but their dinner is not the main object of their lives. So all healthily minded people like making money—ought to like it, and to enjoy the sensation of winning it; but the main object of their life is not money; it is something better than money. A good soldier, for instance, mainly wishes to do his fighting well. He is glad of his pay—very properly so, and justly grumbles when you keep him ten years without it—still, his main notion of life is to win battles, not to be paid for winning them. So of clergymen. They like pew-rents, and baptismal fees, of course; but yet, if they are brave and well educated, the pew-rent is not the sole object of their lives, and the baptismal fee is not the sole purpose of the baptism; the clergyman's object is essentially to baptize and preach, not to be paid for preaching. So of doctors. They like fees no doubt,—ought to like them; yet if they are brave and well educated, the entire object of their lives is not fees. They, on the whole, desire to cure the sick; and,—if they are good doctors, and the choice were fairly put to them,—would rather cure their patient, and lose their fee, than kill him, and get it. And so with all other brave and rightly trained men; their work is first, their fee second—very important always, but still *second*. But in every nation, as I said, there are a vast class who are ill-educated, cowardly, and more or less stupid. And with these people, just as certainly the fee is first, and the work second, as with brave people the work is first and the fee second. And this is no small distinction. It is the whole distinction in a man; distinction between life and death *in* him, between heaven and hell *for* him. You cannot serve two masters;—you *must* serve one or other. If your work is first with you, and your fee second, work is your master, and the lord of work, who is God. But if your fee is first with you, and your work second, fee is your master, and the lord of fee, who is the Devil; and not only the Devil, but the lowest of devils—the "least erected fiend that fell." So there you have it in brief terms; Work first —you are God's servants; Fee first—you are the Fiend's. And it makes a difference, now and ever, believe me, whether you serve Him who has on His vesture and thigh written, "King of Kings," and whose service is perfect freedom; or him on whose vesture and thigh the name is written, "Slave of Slaves," and whose service is perfect slavery.

However, in every nation there are, and must always be, a certain number of these Fiend's servants, who have it principally for the object of their lives to make money.

They are always, as I said, more or less stupid, and cannot conceive of anything else so nice as money. Stupidity is always the basis of the Judas bargain. We do great injustice to Iscariot, in thinking him wicked above all common wickedness. He was only a common money-lover, and, like all money-lovers, didn't understand Christ;—couldn't make out the worth of Him, or meaning of Him. He didn't want Him to be killed. He was horror-struck when he found that Christ would be killed; threw his money away instantly, and hanged himself. How many of our present money-seekers, think you, would have the grace to hang themselves, whoever was killed? But Judas was a common, selfish, muddle-headed, pilfering fellow; his hand always in the bag of the poor, not caring for them. He didn't understand Christ;—yet believed in Him, much more than most of us do; had seen Him do miracles, thought He was quite strong enough to shift for Himself, and he, Judas, might as well make his own little bye-perquisites out of the affair. Christ would come out of it well enough, and he have his thirty pieces. Now, that is the money-seeker's idea, all over the world. He doesn't hate Christ, but can't understand Him—doesn't care for him—sees no good in that benevolent business; makes his own little job out of it at all events, come what will. And thus, out of every mass of men, you have a certain number of bag-men—your "fee-first" men, whose main object is to make money. And they do make it—make it in all sorts of unfair ways, chiefly by the weight and force of money itself, or what is called the power of capital; that is to say, the power which money, once obtained, has over the labor of the poor, so that the capitalist can take all its produce to himself, except the laborer's food. That is the modern Judas's way of "carrying the bag," and "bearing what is put therein."

Nay, but (it is asked) how is that an unfair advantage? Has not the man who has worked for the money a right to use it as he best can? No; in this respect, money is now exactly what mountain promontories over public roads were in old times. The barons fought for them fairly:— the strongest and cunningest got them; then fortified them, and made everyone who passed below pay toll. Well, capital now is exactly what crags were then. Men fight fairly (we will, at least, grant so much, though it is more than we ought) for their money; but, once having got it, the fortified millionaire can make everybody who passes below pay toll to his million, and build another tower of his money castle. And I can tell you, the poor vagrants by the roadside suffer now quite as much from the bag-baron, as ever they did from the crag-baron. Bags and crags have just the same result on rags. I have not time, however, to-night to show you in how many ways the power of capital is unjust; but this one great principle I have to assert—you will find it quite indisputably true—that whenever money is the principal object of life with either man or nation, it is both got ill, and spent ill; and does harm both in the getting and spending; but when it is not the principal object, it and all other things will be well got, and well spent. And here is the test, with every man, of whether money is the principal object with him, or not. If in mid-life he could pause and say, "Now I have enough to live upon, I'll live upon it; and having well earned it, I will also well spend it, and go out of the world poor, as I came into it," then money is not principal with him; but if, having enough to live upon in the manner befitting his character and rank, he still wants to make more, and to *die* rich, then money is the principal object with him, and it becomes a curse to himself, and generally to those who spend it after him. For you know it *must* be spent some day; the only question is whether the man who makes it shall spend it, or some one else. And generally it is better for the maker to spend it, for he will know best its value and use. This is the true law of life. And if a man does not choose thus to spend his money, he must either hoard it or lend it, and the worst thing he can generally do is to lend it; for borrowers are nearly always ill-spenders, and it is with lent money that all evil is mainly done, and all unjust war protracted.

For observe what the real fact is, respecting loans to foreign military governments, and how strange it is. If your little boy came to you to ask for money to spend in squibs and crackers, you would think twice before you gave it him; and you would have some idea that it was wasted, when you saw it fly off in fireworks, even though he did no mischief with it. But the Russian children, and Austrian children, come to you, borrowing money, not to spend in innocent squibs, but in cartridges and bayonets to attack you in India with, and to keep down all noble life in Italy with, and to murder Polish women and children with; and *that* you will give at once, because they pay you interest for it. Now, in order to pay you that interest, they must tax every working peasant in their dominions; and on that work you live. You, therefore, at once rob the Austrian peasant, assassinate or banish the Polish peasant, and you live on the produce of the theft, and the bribe for the assassination! That is the broad fact—that is the practical meaning of your foreign loans, and of most large interest of money; and then you quarrel with Bishop Colenso, forsooth, as if *he* denied the Bible, and you believed it! though, wretches as you are, every deliberate act of your lives is a new defiance of its primary orders; and as if, for most of the rich men of England at this moment, it were not indeed to be desired, as the best thing at least for *them*, that the Bible should *not* be true, since against them these words are written in it: "The rust of your gold and silver shall be a witness against you, and shall eat your flesh, as it were fire."

III. I pass now to our third condition of separation, between the men who work with the hand, and those who work with the head.

And here we have at last an inevitable distinction. There *must* be work done by the arms, or none of us could live. There *must* be work done by the brains, or the life we get would not be worth having. And the same men cannot do both. There is rough work to be done, and rough men must do it; there is gentle work to be done, and gentlemen must do it; and it is physically impossible that one class should do, or divide, the work of the other. And it is of no use to try to conceal this sorrowful fact by fine words, and to talk to the workman about the honorableness of manual labor, and the dignity of humanity. That is a grand old proverb of Sancho Panza's, "Fine words butter no parsnips;" and I can tell you that, all over England just now, you workmen are buying a great deal too much butter at that dairy. Rough work, honorable or not, takes the life out of us; and the man who has been heaving clay out of a ditch all day, or driving an express train against the north wind all night, or holding a collier's helm in a gale on a lee-shore, or whirling white hot iron at a furnace mouth, that man is not the same at the end of his day, or night, as one who has been sitting in a quiet room, with everything comfortable about him, reading books, or classing butterflies, or painting pictures. If it is any comfort to you to be told that the rough work is the more honorable of the two, I should be sorry to take that much of consolation from you; and in some sense I need not. The rough work is at all events real, honest, and, generally, though not always, useful; while the fine work is, a great deal of it, foolish and false as well as fine, and therefore dishonorable; but when both kinds are equally well and worthily done, the head's is the noble work, and the hand's the ignoble; and of all hand work whatsoever, necessary for the maintenance of life, those old words, "In the sweat of thy face thou shalt eat bread," indicate that the inherent nature of it is one of calamity; and that the ground, cursed for our sake, casts also some shadow of degradation into our contest with its thorn and its thistle; so that all nations have held their days honorable, or "holy," and constituted them "holydays" or "holidays," by making them days of rest; and the promise, which, among all our distant hopes, seems to cast the chief brightness over death, is that blessing of the dead who die in the Lord, that "they rest from their labors, and their works do follow them."

And thus the perpetual question and contest must arise, who is to do this rough work? and how is the worker of it to be comforted, redeemed, and rewarded? and what kind of play should he have, and what rest, in this world, sometimes, as well as in the next? Well, my good working friends, these questions will take a little time to answer yet. They must be answered: all good men are occupied with them, and all honest thinkers. There's grand head work doing about them; but much must be discovered, and much attempted in vain, before anything decisive can be told you. Only note these few particulars, which are already sure.

As to the distribution of the hard work. None of us, or very few of us, do either hard or soft work because we

think we ought; but because we have chanced to fall into
the way of it, and cannot help ourselves. Now, nobody
does anything well that they cannot help doing: work is
only done well when it is done with a will; and no man
has a thoroughly sound will unless he knows he is doing
what he should, and is in his place. And, depend upon it,
all work must be done at last, not in a disorderly, scram-
bling, doggish way, but in an ordered, soldierly, human
way—a lawful way. Men are enlisted for the labor that
kills—the labor of war: they are counted, trained, fed,
dressed, and praised for that. Let them be enlisted also
for the labor that feeds: let them be counted, trained, fed,
dressed, praised for that. Teach the plow exercise as
carefully as you do the sword exercise, and let the officers
of troops of life be held as much gentlemen as the officers
of troops of death; and all is done: but neither this, nor
any other right thing, can be accomplished—you can't
even see your way to it—unless, first of all, both servant
and master are resolved that, come what will of it, they will
do each other justice. People are perpetually squabbling
about what will be best to do, or easiest to do, or advise-
ablest to do, or profitablest to do; but they never, so far
as I hear them talk, ever ask what it is *just* to do. And
it is the law of heaven that you shall not be able to judge
what is wise or easy, unless you are first resolved to judge
what is just, and to do it. That is the one thing constantly
reiterated by our Master—the order of all others that is
given oftenest—"Do justice and judgment." That's your
Bible order; that's the "Service of God," not praying nor
psalm-singing. You are told, indeed, to sing psalms when
you are merry, and to pray when you need anything; and,
by the perversion of the Evil Spirit, we get to think that
praying and psalm-singing are "service." If a child finds

itself in want of anything, it runs in and asks its father for it—does it call that, doing its father a service? If it begs for a toy or a piece of cake—does it call that serving its father? That, with God, is prayer, and He likes to hear it: He likes you to ask Him for cake when you want it; but He doesn't call that "serving Him." Begging is not serving: God likes mere beggars as little as you do—He likes honest servants, not beggars. So when a child loves its father very much, and is very happy, it may sing little songs about him; but it doesn't call that serving its father; neither is singing songs about God, serving God. It is enjoying ourselves, if it's anything; most probably it is nothing; but if it's anything, it is serving ourselves, not God. And yet we are impudent enough to call our beggings and chantings "Divine Service:" we say "Divine service will be 'performed'" (that's our word—the form of it gone through) "at eleven o'clock." Alas!—unless we perform Divine service in every willing act of our life, we never perform it at all. The one Divine work—the one ordered sacrifice—is to do justice; and it is the last we are ever inclined to do. Anything rather than that! As much charity as you choose, but no justice. "Nay," you will say, "charity is greater than justice." Yes, it is greater; it is the summit of justice—it is the temple of which justice is the foundation. But you can't have the top without the bottom; you cannot build upon charity. You must build upon justice, for this main reason, that you have not, at first, charity to build with. It is the last reward of good work. Do justice to your brother (you can do that, whether you love him or not), and you will come to love him. But do injustice to him, because you don't love him; and you will come to hate him. It is all very fine to think you can build upon charity to begin with; but you will find all you have got to begin with, begins at home, and is essentially love of yourself. You well-to-do people, for instance, who are here to-night, will go to "Divine service" next Sunday, all nice and tidy, and your little children will have their tight little Sunday boots on, and lovely little Sunday feathers in their hats; and you'll think, complacently and piously, how lovely they look! So they do: and you love them heartily, and you like sticking feathers in their hats. That's all right: that *is* charity; but it is charity beginning at home. Then you will come to the poor little crossing-sweeper, got up also,—it, in its Sunday dress,—the dirtiest rags it has,— that it may beg the better: we shall give it a penny, and think how good we are. That's charity going abroad. But what does Justice say, walking and watching near us? Christian Justice has been strangely mute, and seemingly blind; and, if not blind, decrepit, this many a day: she keeps her accounts still, however—quite steadily—doing them at nights, carefully, with her bandage off, and through acutest spectacles (the only modern scientific invention she cares about). You must put your ear down ever so close to her lips to hear her speak; and then you will start at what she first whispers, for it will certainly be, "Why shouldn't that little crossing-sweeper have a feather on its head, as well as your own child?" Then you may ask Justice, in an amazed manner, "How she can possibly be so foolish as to think children could sweep crossings with feathers on their heads?" Then you stoop again, and Justice says—still in her dull, stupid way—"Then, why don't you, every other Sunday, leave your child to sweep the crossing, and take the little sweeper to church in a hat and feather?" Mercy on us (you think), what will she say next? And you answer, of course, that "you don't, because every body ought to remain content in the position in which Providence has placed them." Ah, my friends, that's the gist of the whole question. *Did* Providence put them in that position, or did *you?* You knock a man into a ditch, and then you tell him to remain content in the "position in which Providence has placed him." That's modern Christianity. You say—"*We* did not knock him into the ditch." How do you know what you have done, or are doing? That's just what we have all got to know, and what we shall never know, until the question with us every morning, is, not how to do the gainful thing, but how to do the just thing; nor until we are at least so far on the way to being Christian, as to have understood that maxim of the poor half-way Mahometan, "One hour in the execution of justice is worth seventy years of prayer."

Supposing, then, we have it determined with appropriate justice, *who* is to do the hand work, the next questions must be how the hand-workers are to be paid, and how they are to be refreshed, and what play they are to have. Now, the possible quantity of play depends on the possible quantity of pay; and the quantity of pay is not a matter for consideration to hand-workers only, but to all workers. Generally, good, useful work, whether of the hand or head, is either ill-paid, or not paid at all. I don't say it should be so, but it always is so. People, as a rule, only pay for being amused or being cheated, not for being served. Five thousand a year to your talker, and a shilling a day to your fighter, digger, and thinker, is the rule. None of the best head work in art, literature, or science, is ever paid for. How much do you think Homer got for his Iliad? or Dante for his Paradise? only bitter bread and salt, and going up and down other people's stairs. In science, the man who discovered the telescope, and first saw heaven, was paid with a dungeon; the man who invented the microscope, and first saw earth, died of starvation, driven from his home: it is indeed very clear that God means all thoroughly good work and talk to be done for nothing. Baruch, the scribe, did not get a penny a line for writing Jeremiah's second roll for him, I fancy; and St. Stephen did not get Bishop's pay for that long sermon of his to the Pharisees; nothing but stones. For indeed that is the world-father's proper payment. So surely as any of the world's children work for the world's good, honestly, with head and heart; and come to it, saying, "Give us a little bread, just to keep the life in us," the world-father answers them, "No, my children, not bread; a stone, if you like, or as many as you need, to keep you quiet." But the hand-workers are not so ill off as all this comes to. The worst that can happen to *you* is to break stones; not be broken by them. And for you there will come a time for better payment; some day, assuredly, more pence will be paid to Peter the Fisherman, and fewer to Peter the Pope; we shall pay people not quite so much for talking in Parliament and doing nothing, as for holding their tongues out of it and doing something; we shall pay our plowman a little more and our lawyer a little less, and so on : but, at least, we may even now take care that whatever work is done shall be fully paid for; and the man who does it paid for it, not somebody else; and that it shall be done in an orderly, soldierly, well-guided, wholesome way, under good captains and lieutenants of labor; and that it shall have its appointed times of rest, and enough of them ; and that in those times the play shall be wholesome play, not in theatrical gardens, with tin flowers and gas sunshine, and girls dancing because of their misery; but in true gardens, with real flowers, and real sunshine, and children dancing because of their gladness; so that truly the streets shall be full (the "streets" mind you, not the gutters) of children, playing in the midst thereof. We may take care that working-men shall have at least as good books to read as anybody else, when they've time to read them; and as comfortable firesides to sit at as anybody else, when they've time to sit at them. This, I think, can be managed for you, my working friends, in the good time.

IV. I must go on, however, to our last head, concerning ourselves all, as workers. What is wise work, and what is foolish work? What the difference between sense and nonsense, in daily occupation?

Well, wise work is, briefly, work *with* God. Foolish work is work *against* God. And work done with God, which He will help, may be briefly described as "Putting in Order"—that is, enforcing God's law of order, spiritual and material, over men and things. The first thing you have to do, essentially, the real "good work," is, with respect to men, to enforce justice, and with respect to things, to enforce tidiness, and fruitfulness. And against these two great human deeds, justice and order, there are perpetually two great demons contending,—the devil of iniquity, or inequity, and the devil of disorder, or of death; for death is only consummation of disorder. You have to fight these two fiends daily. So far as you don't fight against the fiend of iniquity, you work for him. You "work iniquity," and the judgment upon you, for all your "Lord, Lord's," will be "Depart from me, ye that work iniquity." And so far as you do not resist the fiend of disorder, you work disorder, and you yourself do the work of Death, which is sin, and has for its wages, Death himself.

Observe then, all wise work is mainly threefold in character. It is honest, useful, and cheerful.

THE CROWN OF WILD OLIVE. 143

I. It is HONEST. I hardly know anything more strange than that you recognize honesty in play, and you do not in work. In your lightest games, you have always some one to see what you call "fair play." In boxing, you must hit fair; in racing, start fair. Your English watchword is fair-play, your English hatred, foul-play. Did it ever strike you that you wanted another watchword also, fair-work, and another hatred also, foul-work? Your prize-fighter has some honor in him yet; and so have the men in the ring round him: they will judge him to lose the match, by foul hitting. But your prize-merchant gains his match by foul selling, and no one cries out against that. You drive a gambler out of the gambling-room who loads dice, but you leave a tradesman in flourishing business, who loads scales! For observe, all dishonest dealing *is* loading scales. What does it matter whether I get short weight, adulterate substance, or dishonest fabric? The fault in the fabric is incomparably the worst of the two. Give me short measure of food, and I only lose by you; but give me adulterate food, and I die by you. Here, then, is your chief duty, you workmen and tradesmen— to be true to yourselves, and to us who would help you. We can do nothing for you, nor you for yourselves, without honesty. Get that, you get all; without that, your suffrages, your reforms, your free-trade measures, your institutions of science, are all in vain. It is useless to put your heads together, if you can't put your hearts together. Shoulder to shoulder, right hand to right hand, among yourselves, and no wrong hand to anybody else, and you'll win the world yet.

II. Then, secondly, wise work is USEFUL. No man minds, or ought to mind, its being hard, if only it comes to something; but when it is hard, and comes to nothing;

when all our bees' business turns to spiders'; and for honey-comb we have only resultant cobweb, blown away by the next breeze—that is the cruel thing for the worker. Yet do we ever ask ourselves, personally, or even nationally, whether our work is coming to anything or not? We don't care to keep what has been nobly done; still less do we care to do nobly what others would keep; and, least of all, to make the work itself useful instead of deadly to the doer, so as to use his life indeed, but not to waste it. Of all wastes, the greatest waste that you can commit is the waste of labor. If you went down in the morning into your dairy, and you found that your youngest child had got down before you; and that he and the cat were at play together, and that he had poured out all the cream on the floor for the cat to lap up, you would scold the child, and be sorry the milk was wasted. But if, instead of wooden bowls with milk in them, there are golden bowls with human life in them, and instead of the cat to play with— the devil to play with; and you yourself the player; and instead of leaving that golden bowl to be broken by God at the fountain, you break it in the dust yourself, and pour the human blood out on the ground for the fiend to lick up—that is no waste! What! you perhaps think, "to waste the labor of men is not to kill them." Is it not? I should like to know how you could kill them more utterly —kill them with second deaths, seventh deaths, hundred-fold deaths? It is the slightest way of killing to stop a man's breath. Nay, the hunger, and the cold, and the little whistling bullets—our love-messengers between nation and nation—have brought pleasant messages from us to many a man before now; orders of sweet release, and leave at last to go where he will be most welcome and most happy. At the worst you do but shorten his life, you do not corrupt his life. But if you put him to base labor, if you bind his thoughts, if you blind his eyes, if you blunt his hopes, if you steal his joys, if you stunt his body, and blast his soul, and at last leave him not so much as to reap the poor fruit of his degradation, but gather that for yourself, and dismiss him to the grave, when you have done with him, having, so far as in you lay, made the walls of that grave everlasting (though, indeed, I fancy the goodly bricks of some of our family vaults will hold closer in the resurrection day than the sod over the laborer's head), this you think is no waste, and no sin!

III. Then, lastly, wise work is CHEERFUL, as a child's work is. And now I want you to take one thought home with you, and let it stay with you.

Everybody in this room has been taught to pray daily, "Thy kingdom come." Now, if we hear a man swear in the streets, we think it very wrong, and say he "takes God's name in vain." But there's a twenty times worse way of taking His name in vain, than that. It is to *ask God for what we don't want.* He doesn't like that sort of prayer. If you don't want a thing, don't ask for it: such asking is the worst mockery of your King you can mock Him with; the soldiers striking Him on the head with the reed was nothing to that. If you do not wish for His kingdom, don't pray for it. But if you do, you must do more than pray for it; you must work for it. And, to work for it, you must know what it is: we have all prayed for it many a day without thinking. Observe, it is a kingdom that is to come to us; we are not to go to it. Also, it is not to be a kingdom of the dead, but of the living. Also, it is not to come all at once, but quietly; nobody knows how. "The kingdom of God cometh not with observation." Also, it is not to come outside of us, but in the hearts of us: "the kingdom of God is within you." And, being within us, it is not a thing to be seen, but to be felt; and though it brings all substance of good with it, it does not consist in that: "the kingdom of God is not meat and drink, but righteousness, peace, and joy in the Holy Ghost:" joy, that is to say, in the holy, healthful, and helpful Spirit. Now, if we want to work for this kingdom, and to bring it, and enter into it, there's just one condition to be first accepted. You must enter it as children, or not at all; "Whosoever will not receive it as a little child shall not enter therein." And again, "Suffer little children to come unto me, and forbid them not, for of such is the kingdom of heaven."

Of such, observe. Not of children themselves, but of such as children. I believe most mothers who read that text think that all heaven is to be full of babies. But that's not so. There will be children there, but the hoary head is the crown. "Length of days, and long life and peace," that is the blessing, not to die in babyhood. Children die but for their parents' sins; God means them to live, but He can't let them always; then they have their earlier place in heaven: and the little child of David, vainly prayed for;—the little child of Jeroboam, killed by its mother's step on its own threshold,—they will be there. But weary old David, and weary old Barzillai, having learned children's lessons at last, will be there too; and the one question for us all, young or old, is, have we learned our child's lesson? it is the *character* of children we want, and must gain at our peril; let us see, briefly, in what it consists.

The first character of right childhood is that it is Modest. A well-bred child does not think it can teach its parents, or that it knows everything. It may think its father and mother know everything,—perhaps that all grown-up people know everything; very certainly it is sure that *it* does not. And it is always asking questions, and wanting to know more. Well, that is the first character of a good and wise man at his work. To know that he knows very little;—to perceive that there are many above him wiser than he; and to be always asking questions, wanting to learn, not to teach. No one ever teaches well who wants to teach, or governs well who wants to govern; it is an old saying (Plato's, but I know not if his, first), and as wise as old.

Then, the second character of right childhood is to be Faithful. Perceiving that its father knows best what is good for it, and having found always, when it has tried its own way against his, that he was right and it was wrong, a noble child trusts him at last wholly, gives him its hand, and will walk blindfold with him, if he bids it. And that is the true character of all good men also, as obedient workers, or soldiers under captains. They must trust their captains;—they are bound for their lives to choose none but those whom they *can* trust. Then, they are not always to be thinking that what seems strange to them, or wrong in what they are desired to do, *is* strange or wrong. They know their captain: where he leads they must follow, what he bids, they must do; and without this trust and faith, without this captainship and soldiership, no great need, no great salvation, is possible to man. Among all the nations it is only when this faith is attained by them that they become great: the Jew, the Greek, and the Mahometan, agree at least in testifying to this. It was a deed of this absolute trust which made Abraham the father of the faithful; it was the declaration of the power of God as captain over all men, and the acceptance of a leader appointed by Him as commander of the faithful, which laid the foundation of whatever national power yet exists in the East; and the deed of the Greeks, which has become the type of unselfish and noble soldiership to all lands, and to all times, was commemorated, on the tomb of those who gave their lives to do it, in the most pathetic, so far as I know, or can feel, of all human utterances: "Oh, stranger, go and tell our people that we are lying here, having *obeyed* their words."

Then the third character of right childhood is to be Loving and Generous. Give a little love to a child, and you get a great deal back. It loves everything near it, when it is a right kind of child—would hurt nothing, would give the best it has away, always, if you need it—does not lay plans for getting everything in the house for itself, and delights in helping people; you cannot please it so much as by giving it a chance of being useful, in ever so little a way.

And because of all these characters, lastly, it is Cheerful. Putting its trust in its father, it is careful for nothing—being full of love to every creature, it is happy always, whether in its play or in its duty. Well, that's the great worker's character also. Taking no thought for the morrow; taking thought only for the duty of the day; trusting somebody else to take care of to-morrow; knowing indeed what labor is, but not what sorrow is; and always ready for play—beautiful play,—for lovely human play is like the play of the Sun. There's a worker for you. He, steady to his time, is set as a strong man to run his course, but also, he *rejoiceth* as a strong man to run his course. See how he plays in the morning, with the mists below, and the clouds above, with a ray here and a flash there, and a shower of jewels everywhere; that's the

Sun's play; and great human play is like his—all various —all full of light and life, and tender, as the dew of the morning.

So then, you have the child's character in these four things—Humility, Faith, Charity, and Cheerfulness. That's what you have got to be converted to. "Except ye be converted and become as little children"—You hear much of conversion now-a-days; but people always seem to think they have got to be made wretched by conversion,—to be converted to long faces. No, friends, you have got to be converted to short ones; you have to repent into childhood, to repent into delight, and delightsomeness. You can't go into a conventicle but you'll hear plenty of talk of backsliding. Backsliding, indeed! I can tell you, on the ways most of us go, the faster we slide back the better. Slide back into the cradle, if going on is into the grave— back, I tell you; back—out of your long faces, and into your long clothes. It is among children only, and as children only, that you will find medicine for your healing and true wisdom for your teaching. There is poison in the counsels of the *men* of this world; the words they speak are all bitterness, "the poison of asps is under their lips," but, "the sucking child shall play by the hole of the asp." There is death in the looks of men. "Their eyes are privily set against the poor;" they are as the uncharmable serpent, the cockatrice, which slew by seeing. But "the weaned child shall lay his hand on the cockatrice den." There is death in the steps of men: "their feet are swift to shed blood; they have compassed us in our steps like the lion that is greedy of his prey, and the young lion lurking in secret places," but, in that kingdom, the wolf shall lie down with the lamb, and the fatling with the lion, and "a little child shall lead them." There is death in the thoughts of men : the world is one wide riddle to them, darker and darker as it draws to a close ; but the secret of it is known to the child, and the Lord of heaven and earth is most to be thanked in that "He has hidden these things from the wise and prudent, and has revealed them unto babes." Yes, and there is death—infinitude of death in the principalities and powers of men. As far as the east is from the west, so far our sins are—*not* set from us, but multiplied around us : the Sun himself, think you he *now* "rejoices" to run his course, when he plunges westward to the horizon, so widely red, not with clouds, but blood? And it will be red more widely yet. Whatever drought of the early and latter rain may be, there will be none of that red rain. You fortify yourselves, you arm yourselves against it in vain ; the enemy and avenger will be upon you also, unless you learn that it is not out of the mouths of the knitted gun, or the smoothed rifle, but "out of the mouths of babes and sucklings" that the strength is ordained, which shall "still the enemy and avenger."

LECTURE II.

TRAFFIC.

(Delivered in the Town Hall, Bradford.)

MY good Yorkshire friends, you asked me down here among your hills that I might talk to you about this Exchange you are going to build: but earnestly and seriously asking you to pardon me, I am going to do nothing of the kind. I cannot talk, or at least can say very little, about this same Exchange. I must talk of quite other things, though not willingly;—I could not deserve your pardon, if when you invited me to speak on one subject, I willfully spoke on another. But I cannot speak, to purpose, of anything about which I do not care; and most simply and sorrowfully I have to tell you, in the outset, that I do *not* care about this Exchange of yours.

If, however, when you sent me your invitation, I had answered, "I won't come, I don't care about the Exchange of Bradford," you would have been justly offended with me, not knowing the reasons of so blunt a carelessness. So I have come down, hoping that you will patiently let me tell you why, on this, and many other such occasions, I now remain silent, when formerly I should have caught at the opportunity of speaking to a gracious audience.

In a word, then, I do not care about this Exchange,—because *you* don't; and because you know perfectly well I cannot make you. Look at the essential circumstances of the case, which you, as business men, know perfectly well, though perhaps you think I forget them. You are going to spend £30,000, which to you, collectively, is nothing; the buying a new coat is, as to the cost of it, a much more important matter of consideration to me than building a new Exchange is to you. But you think you may as well have the right thing for your money. You know there are a great many odd styles of architecture about; you don't want to do anything ridiculous; you hear of me, among others, as a respectable architectural man-milliner: and you send for me, that I may tell you the leading fashion; and what is, in our shops, for the moment, the newest and sweetest thing in pinnacles.

Now, pardon me for telling you frankly, you cannot have good architecture merely by asking people's advice on occasion. All good architecture is the expression of national life and character; and it is produced by a prevalent and eager national taste, or desire for beauty. And I want you to think a little of the deep significance of this word "taste;" for no statement of mine has been more earnestly or oftener controverted than that good taste is essentially a moral quality. "No," say many of my antagonists, "taste is one thing, morality is another. Tell us what is pretty; we shall be glad to know that; but preach no sermons to us."

Permit me, therefore, to fortify this old dogma of mine somewhat. Taste is not only a part and an index of morality—it is the ONLY morality. The first, and last, and closest trial question to any living creature is, "What do you like?" Tell me what you like, and I'll tell you what you are. Go out into the street, and ask the first man or woman you meet, what their "taste" is, and if they answer candidly, you know them, body and soul. "You, my friend in the rags, with the unsteady gait, what do *you* like?" "A pipe and a quartern of gin." I know you. "You, good woman, with the quick step and tidy bonnet, what do you like?" "A swept hearth and a clean tea-table, and my husband opposite me, and a baby at my breast." Good, I know you also. "You, little girl with the golden hair and the soft eyes, what do you like?" "My canary, and a run among the wood hyacinths." "You, little boy with the dirty hands and the low forehead, what do you like?" "A shy at the sparrows, and a game at pitch-farthing." Good; we know them all now. What more need we ask?

"Nay," perhaps you answer: "we need rather to ask what these people and children do, than what they like. If they *do* right, it is no matter that they like what is wrong; and if they *do* wrong, it is no matter that they like what is right. Doing is the great thing; and it does not matter that the man likes drinking, so that he does not drink; nor that the little girl likes to be kind to her canary, if she will not learn her lessons; nor that the little boy likes throwing stones at the sparrows, if he goes to the Sunday school." Indeed, for a short time, and in a provisional sense, this is true. For if, resolutely, people do what is right, in time they come to like doing it. But they only are in a right moral state when they *have* come to like doing it; and as long as they don't like it, they are still in a vicious state. The man is not in health of body who is always thirsting for the bottle in the cupboard, though he bravely bears his thirst; but the man who heartily enjoys water in the morning and wine in the evening, each in its proper quantity and time. And the entire object of true education is to make people not merely *do* the right things, but *enjoy* the right things—not merely industrious, but to love industry—not merely learned, but to love knowledge—not merely pure, but to love purity—not merely just, but to hunger and thirst after justice.

But you may answer or think; "Is the liking for outside ornaments,—for pictures, or statues, or furniture, or architecture,—a moral quality?" Yes, most surely, if a rightly set liking. Taste for *any* pictures or statues is not a moral quality, but taste for good ones is. Only here again we have to define the word "good." I don't mean by "good," clever—or learned—or difficult in the doing. Take a picture by Teniers, of sots quarreling over their dice: it is an entirely clever picture; so clever that nothing in its kind has ever been done equal to it; but it is also an entirely base and evil picture. It is an expression of delight in the prolonged contemplation of a vile thing, and delight in that is an "unmannered," or "immoral" quality. It is "bad taste" in the profoundest sense—it is the taste of the devils. On the other hand, a picture of Titian's, or a Greek statue, or a Greek coin, or a Turner landscape, expresses delight in the perpetual contemplation of a good and perfect thing. That is an entirely moral quality—it is the taste of the angels. And all delight in art, and all love of it, resolve themselves into simple love of that which deserves love. That deserving is the quality which we call "loveliness"— (we ought to have an opposite word, hateliness, to be said of the things which deserve to be hated); and it is not an indifferent nor optional thing whether we love this or that; but it is just the vital function of all our being. What we *like* determines what we *are*, and is the sign of what we are; and to teach taste is inevitably to form character. As I was thinking over this, in walking up Fleet Street the other day, my eye caught the title of a book standing open in a bookseller's window. It was—"On the necessity of the diffusion of taste among all classes." "Ah," I thought to myself, "my classifying friend, when you have diffused your taste, where will your classes be? The man who likes what you like, belongs to the same class with you, I think. Inevitably so. You may put him to other work if you choose; but, by the condition you have brought him into, he will dislike the other work as much as you would yourself. You get hold of a scavenger, or a costermonger, who enjoyed the Newgate Calendar for literature, and 'Pop goes the Weasel' for music. You think you can make him like Dante and Beethoven? I wish you joy of your lessons; but if you do, you have made a gentleman of him:—he won't like to go back to his costermongering."

And so completely and unexceptionally is this so, that, if I had time to-night, I could show you that a nation cannot be affected by any vice, or weakness, without expressing it, legibly, and for ever, either in bad art, or by want of art; and that there is no national virtue, small or great, which is not manifestly expressed in all the art which circumstances enable the people possessing that virtue to produce. Take, for instance, your great English virtue of enduring and patient courage. You have at present in England only one art of any consequence—that is, ironworking. You know thoroughly well how to cast and hammer iron. Now, do you think in those masses of lava which you build volcanic cones to melt, and which you forge at the mouths of the Infernos you have created; do you think, on those iron plates, your courage and endurance are not written for ever—not merely with an iron pen, but on iron parchment? And take also your great English vice—European vice—vice of all the world —vice of all other worlds that roll or shine in heaven, bearing with them yet the atmosphere of hell—the vice of jealousy, which brings competition into your commerce, treachery into your councils, and dishonor into your wars —that vice which has rendered for you, and for your next neighboring nation, the daily occupations of existence no longer possible, but with the mail upon your breasts and the sword loose in its sheath; so that, at last, you have realized for all the multitudes of the two great peoples who lead the so-called civilization of the earth,—you have realized for them all, I say, in person and in policy, what was once true only of the rough Border riders of your Cheviot hills—

> "They carved at the meal
> With gloves of steel,
> And they drank the red wine through the helmet barr'd ;—

do you think that this national shame and dastardliness of heart are not written as legibly on every rivet of your iron armor as the strength of the right hands that forged it? Friends, I know not whether this thing be the more ludicrous or the more melancholy. It is quite unspeakably both. Suppose, instead of being now sent for by you, I had been sent for by some private gentleman, living in a suburban house, with his garden separated only by a fruit-wall from his next door neighbor's; and he had called me to consult with him on the furnishing of his drawing room. I begin looking about me, and find the walls rather bare; I think such and such a paper might be desirable—perhaps a little fresco here and there on the ceiling—a damask curtain or so at the windows. "Ah," says my employer, "damask curtains indeed! That's all very fine, but you know I can't afford that kind of thing just now!" "Yet the world credits you with a splendid income!" "Ah, yes," says my friend, "but do you know, at present, I am obliged to spend it nearly all in steel-traps?" "Steel-traps! for whom?" "Why, for that fellow on the other side the wall, you know: we're very good friends, capital friends;

but we are obliged to keep our traps set on both sides of the wall; we could not possibly keep on friendly terms without them, and our spring guns. The worst of it is, we are both clever fellows enough; and there's never a day passes that we don't find out a new trap, or a new gun-barrel, or something; we spend about fifteen millions a year each in our traps, take it all together; and I don't see how we're to do with less." A highly comic state of life for two private gentlemen! but for two nations, it seems to me, not wholly comic? Bedlam would be comic, perhaps, if there were only one madman in it; and your Christmas pantomime is comic, when there is only one clown in it; but when the whole world turns clown, and paints itself red with its own heart's blood instead of vermilion, it is something else than comic, I think.

Mind, I know a great deal of this is play, and willingly allow for that. You don't know what to do with yourselves for a sensation: fox-hunting and cricketing will not carry you through the whole of this unendurably long mortal life: you liked pop-guns when you were schoolboys, and rifles and Armstrongs are only the same things better made: but then the worst of it is, that what was play to you when boys, was not play to the sparrows; and what is play to you now, is not play to the small birds of State neither; and for the black eagles, you are somewhat shy of taking shots at them, if I mistake not.

I must get back to the matter in hand, however. Believe me, without further instance, I could show you, in all time, that every nation's vice, or virtue, was written in its art: the soldiership of early Greece; the sensuality of late Italy; the visionary religion of Tuscany; the splendid human energy and beauty of Venice. I have no time to do this to-night (I have done it elsewhere before now);

but I proceed to apply the principle to ourselves in a more searching manner.

I notice that among all the new buildings that cover your once wild hills, churches and schools are mixed in due, that is to say, in large proportion, with your mills and mansions; and I notice also that the churches and schools are almost always Gothic, and the mansions and mills are never Gothic. Will you allow me to ask precisely the meaning of this? For, remember, it is peculiarly a modern phenomenon. When Gothic was invented, houses were Gothic as well as churches; and when the Italian style superseded the Gothic, churches were Italian as well as houses. If there is a Gothic spire to the cathedral of Antwerp, there is a Gothic belfry to the Hôtel de Ville at Brussels; if Inigo Jones builds an Italian Whitehall, Sir Chistopher Wren builds an Italian St. Paul's. But now you live under one school of architecture, and worship under another. What do you mean by doing this? Am I to understand that you are thinking of changing your architecture back to Gothic; and that you treat your churches experimentally, because it does not matter what mistakes you make in a church? Or am I to understand that you consider Gothic a pre-eminently sacred and beautiful mode of building, which you think, like the fine frankincense, should be mixed for the tabernacle only, and reserved for your religious services? For if this be the feeling, though it may seem at first as if it were graceful and reverent, you will find that, at the root of the matter, it signifies neither more nor less than that you have separated your religion from your life.

For consider what a wide significance this fact has; and remember that it is not you only, but all the people of England, who are behaving thus just now.

You have all got into the habit of calling the church "the house of God." I have seen, over the doors of many churches, the legend actually carved, "*This* is the house of God, and this is the gate of heaven." Now, note where that legend comes from, and of what place it was first spoken. A boy leaves his father's house to go on a long journey on foot, to visit his uncle; he has to cross a wild hill-desert; just as if one of your own boys had to cross the wolds of Westmoreland, to visit an uncle at Carlisle. The second or third day your boy finds himself somewhere between Hawes and Brough, in the midst of the moors, at sunset. It is stony ground, and boggy; he cannot go one foot further that night. Down he lies, to sleep, on Wharnside, where best he may, gathering a few of the stones together to put under his head;—so wild the place is, he cannot get anything but stones. And there, lying under the broad night, he has a dream; and he sees a ladder set up on the earth, and the top of it reaches to heaven, and the angels of God are ascending and descending upon it. And when he wakes out of his sleep, he says, "How dreadful is this place; surely, this is none other than the house of God, and this is the gate of heaven." This PLACE, observe; not this church; not this city; not this stone, even, which he puts up for a memorial—the piece of flint on which his head has lain. But this *place;* this windy slope of Wharnside; this moorland hollow, torrent-bitten, snow-blighted; this *any* place where God lets down the ladder. And how are you to know where that will be? or how are you to determine where it may be, but by being ready for it always? Do you know where the lightning is to fall next? You *do* know that, partly; you can guide the lightning; but you cannot guide the going forth of the Spirit, which is that lightning when it shines from the east to the west.

But the perpetual and insolent warping of that strong verse to serve a merely ecclesiastical purpose, is only one of the thousand instances in which we sink back into gross Judaism. We call our churches "temples." Now, you know, or ought to know, they are *not* temples. They have never had, never can have, anything whatever to do with temples. They are "synagogues"—"gathering places"— where you gather yourselves together as an assembly; and by not calling them so, you again miss the force of another mighty text—"Thou, when thou prayest, shalt not be as the hypocrites are; for they love to pray standing in the *churches*" [we should translate it], "that they may be seen of men. But thou, when thou prayest, enter into thy closet, and when thou hast shut thy door, pray to thy Father,"— which is, not in chancel nor in aisle, but "in secret."

Now, you feel, as I say this to you—I know you feel— as if I were trying to take away the honor of your churches. Not so; I am trying to prove to you the honor of your houses and your hills; I am trying to show you—not that the Church is not sacred—but that the whole Earth is. I would have you feel, what careless, what constant, what infectious sin there is in all modes of thought, whereby, in calling your churches only "holy," you call your hearths and homes profane; and have separated yourselves from the heathen by casting all your household gods to the ground, instead of recognizing, in the place of their many and feeble Lares, the presence of your One and Mighty Lord and Lar.

"But what has all this to do with our Exchange?" you ask me, impatiently. My dear friends, it has just everything to do with it; on these inner and great questions depend all the outer and little ones; and if you have asked me down here to speak to you, because you had before been interested in anything I have written, you must know that all I have yet said about architecture was to show this. The book I called "The Seven Lamps" was to show that certain right states of temper and moral feeling were the magic powers by which all good architecture, without exception, had been produced. "The Stones of Venice," had, from beginning to end, no other aim than to show that the Gothic architecture of Venice had arisen out of, and indicated in all its features, a state of pure national faith, and of domestic virtue; and that its Renaissance architecture had arisen out of, and in all its features indicated, a state of concealed national infidelity, and of domestic corruption. And now, you ask me what style is best to build in; and how can I answer, knowing the meaning of the two styles, but by another question—do you mean to build as Christians or as Infidels? And still more—do you mean to build as honest Christians or as honest Infidels? as thoroughly and confessedly either one or the other? You don't like to be asked such rude questions. I cannot help it; they are of much more importance than this Exchange business; and if they can be at once answered, the Exchange business settles itself in a moment. But, before I press them further, I must ask leave to explain one point clearly. In all my past work, my endeavor has been to show that good architecture is essentially religious—the production of a faithful and virtuous, not of an infidel and corrupted people. But in the course of doing this, I have had also to show that good architecture is not *ecclesiastical*. People are so apt to look upon religion as the business of the clergy, not their own, that the moment they hear of anything depending on "religion," they think it must also have depended on the priesthood; and I have had to take what place was to be occupied between these two errors, and fight both, often with seeming contradiction. Good architecture is the work of good and believing men ; therefore, you say, at least some people say, "Good architecture must essentially have been the work of the clergy, not of the laity." No—a thousand times no ; good architecture has always been the work of the commonalty, *not* of the clergy. What, you say, those glorious cathedrals—the pride of Europe—did their builders not form Gothic architecture? No; they corrupted Gothic architecture. Gothic was formed in the baron's castle, and the burgher's street. It was formed by the thoughts, and hands, and powers of free citizens and soldier kings. By the monk it was used as an instrument for the aid of his superstition ; when that superstition became a beautiful madness, and the best hearts of Europe vainly dreamed and pined in the cloister, and vainly raged and perished in the crusade—through that fury of perverted faith and wasted war, the Gothic rose also to its loveliest, most fantastic, and, finally, most foolish dreams ; and, in those dreams, was lost.

I hope, now, that there is no risk of your misunderstanding me when I come to the gist of what I want to say to-night—when I repeat, that every great national architecture has been the result and exponent of a great national religion. You can't have bits of it here, bits there—you must have it everywhere, or nowhere. It is not the monopoly of a clerical company—it is not the exponent of a theological dogma—it is not the hieroglyphic writing of an initiated priesthood ; it is the manly language of a people inspired by resolute and common purpose, and rendering resolute and common fidelity to the legible laws of an undoubted God.

Now, there have as yet been three distinct schools of European architecture. I say, European, because Asiatic and African architectures belong so entirely to other races and climates, that there is no question of them here; only, in passing, I will simply assure you that whatever is good or great in Egypt, and Syria, and India, is just good or great for the same reasons as the buildings on our side of the Bosphorus. We Europeans, then, have had three great religions: the Greek, which was the worship of the God of Wisdom and Power; the Mediæval, which was the Worship of the God of Judgment and Consolation; the Renaissance, which was the worship of the God of Pride and Beauty; these three we have had—they are past,—and now, at last, we English have got a fourth religion, and a God of our own, about which I want to ask you. But I must explain these three old ones first.

I repeat, first, the Greeks essentially worshiped the God of Wisdom; so that whatever contended against their religion,—to the Jews a stumbling block,—was, to the Greeks—*Foolishness*.

The first Greek idea of Deity was that expressed in the word, of which we keep the remnant in our words "*Di*-urnal" and "*Di*-vine."—the god of *Day*, Jupiter the revealer. Athena is his daughter, but especially daughter of the Intellect, springing armed from the head. We are only with the help of recent investigation beginning to penetrate the depth of meaning couched under the Athenaic symbols: but I may note rapidly, that her ægis, the mantle with the serpent fringes, in which she often, in the best statues, is represented as folding up her left hand for better guard, and the Gorgon on her shield, are both representative mainly of the chilling horror and sadness (turning men to stone, as it were), of the outmost and superficial spheres of knowledge—that knowledge which separates, in bitterness, hardness, and sorrow the heart of the full-grown man from the heart of the child. For out of imperfect knowledge spring terror, dissension, danger, and disdain; but from perfect knowledge, given by the full-revealed Athena, strength and peace, in sign of which she is crowned with the olive spray, and bears the resistless spear.

This, then, was the Greek's conception of purest Deity, and every habit of life, and every form of his art developed themselves from the seeking this bright, serene, resistless wisdom; and setting himself, as a man, to do things evermore rightly and strongly;* not with any ardent affection or ultimate hope; but with a resolute and continent energy of will, as knowing that for failure there was no consolation, and for sin there was no remission. And the Greek architecture rose unerring, bright, clearly defined, and self-contained.

Next followed in Europe the great Christian faith, which was essentially the religion of Comfort. Its great doctrine is the remission of sins; for which cause it happens, too often, in certain phases of Christianity, that sin and sickness themselves are partly glorified, as if, the more you had to be healed of, the more divine was the healing. The practical result of this doctrine, in art, is a continual contemplation of sin and disease, and of imaginary states of purification from them; thus we have an architecture conceived in a mingled sentiment of melancholy and aspiration, partly severe, partly luxuriant, which will bend itself to

---

* It is an error to suppose that the Greek worship, or seeking, was chiefly of Beauty. It was essentially of Rightness and Strength, founded on Forethought: the principal character of Greek art is not Beauty, but Design: and the Dorian Apollo-worship and Athenian Virgin-worship are both expressions of adoration of divine Wisdom and Purity. Next to these great deities rank, in power over the national mind, Dionysus and Ceres, the givers of human strength and life: then, for heroic example, Hercules. There is no Venus-worship among the Greeks in the great times: and the Muses are essentially teachers of Truth, and of its harmonies.

every one of our needs, and every one of our fancies, and be strong or weak with us, as we are strong or weak ourselves. It is, of all architecture, the basest, when base people build it—of all, the noblest, when built by the noble.

And now note that both these religions—Greek and Mediæval—perished by falsehood in their own main purpose. The Greek religion of Wisdom perished in a false philosophy—"Oppositions of science, falsely so called." The Mediæval religion of Consolation perished in false comfort; in remission of sins given lyingly. It was the selling of absolution that ended the Mediæval faith; and I can tell you more, it is the selling of absolution which, to the end of time, will mark false Christianity. Pure Christianity gives her remission of sins only by *ending* them; but false Christianity gets her remission of sins by *compounding for* them. And there are many ways of compounding for them. We English have beautiful little quiet ways of buying absolution, whether in low Church or high, far more cunning than any of Tetzel's trading.

Then, thirdly, there followed the religion of Pleasure, in which all Europe gave itself to luxury, ending in death. First, *bals masqués* in every saloon, and then guillotines in every square. And all these three worships issue in vast temple building. Your Greek worshiped Wisdom, and built you the Parthenon—the Virgin's temple. The Mediæval worshiped Consolation, and built you Virgin temples also—but to our Lady of Salvation. Then the Revivalist worshiped beauty, of a sort, and built you Versailles, and the Vatican. Now, lastly, will you tell me what *we* worship, and what *we* build?

You know we are speaking always of the real, active, continual, national worship; that by which men act while they live; not that which they talk of when they die. Now, we have, indeed, a nominal religion, to which we pay tithes of property, and sevenths of time; but we have also a practical and earnest religion, to which we devote nine-tenths of our property and six-sevenths of our time. And we dispute a great deal about the nominal religion; but we are all unanimous about this practical one, of which I think you will admit that the ruling goddess may be best generally described as the "Goddess of Getting-on," or "Britannia of the Market." The Athenians had an "Athena Agoraia," or Minerva of the Market; but she was a subordinate type of their goddess, while our Britannia Agoraia is the principal type of ours. And all your great architectural works are, of course, built to her. It is long since you built a great cathedral; and how you would laugh at me, if I proposed building a cathedral on the top of one of these hills of yours, taking it for an Acropolis! But your railroad mounds, prolonged masses of Acropolis; your railroad stations, vaster than the Parthenon, and innumerable; your chimneys, how much more mighty and costly than cathedral spires! your harbor-piers; your warehouses; your exchanges!—all these are built to your great Goddess of "Getting-on;" and she has formed, and will continue to form, your architecture, as long as you worship her; and it is quite vain to ask me to tell you how to build to *her;* you know far better than I.

There might indeed, on some theories, be a conceivably good architecture for Exchanges—that is to say if there were any heroism in the fact or deed of exchange, which might be typically carved on the outside of your building. For, you know, all beautiful architecture must be adorned with sculpture or painting; and for sculpture or painting, you must have a subject. And hitherto it has been a received opinion among the nations of the world that the only right subjects for either, were *heroisms* of some sort. Even on his pots and his flagons, the Greek put a Hercules slaying lions, or an Apollo slaying serpents, or Bacchus slaying melancholy giants, and earth-born despondencies. On his temples, the Greek put contests of great warriors in founding states, or of gods with evil spirits. On his houses and temples alike, the Christian put carvings of angels conquering devils; or of hero-martyrs exchanging this world for another; subject inappropriate, I think, to our manner of exchange here. And the Master of Christians not only left his followers without any orders as to the sculpture of affairs of exchange on the outside of buildings, but gave some strong evidence of his dislike of affairs of exchange within them. And yet there might surely be a heroism in such affairs; and all commerce become a kind of selling of doves, not impious. The wonder has always been great to me, that heroism has never been supposed to be in anywise consistent with the practice of supplying people with food, or clothes; but rather with that of quartering oneself upon them for food, and stripping them of their clothes. Spoiling of armor is an heroic deed in all ages; but the selling of clothes, old, or new, has never taken any color of magnanimity. Yet one does not see why feeding the hungry and clothing the naked should ever become base businesses, even when engaged in on a large scale. If one could contrive to attach the notion of conquest to them anyhow? so that, supposing there were anywhere an obstinate race, who refused to be comforted, one might take some pride in giving them compulsory comfort; and as it were, "occupying a country" with one's gifts, instead of one's armies? If one could only consider it as much a victory to get a barren field sown, as to get an eared field stripped; and contend who should build villages, instead of who should "carry" them. Are not all forms of heroism conceivable in doing these serviceable deeds? You doubt who is strongest? It might be ascertained by push of spade, as well as push of sword. Who is wisest? There are witty things to be thought of in planning other business than campaigns. Who is bravest? There are always the elements to fight with, stronger than men; and nearly as merciless. The only absolutely and unapproachably heroic element in the soldier's work seems to be—that he is paid little for it—and regularly: while you traffickers, and exchangers, and others occupied in presumably benevolent business, like to be paid much for it—and by chance. I never can make out how it is that a knight-errant does not expect to be paid for his trouble, but a pedlar-errant always does;—that people are willing to take hard knocks for nothing, but never to sell ribbons cheap;—that they are ready to go on fervent crusades to recover the tomb of a buried God, never on any travels to fulfill the orders of a living God;—that they will go anywhere barefoot to preach their faith, but must be well bribed to practice it, and are perfectly ready to give the Gospel gratis, but never the loaves and fishes. If you chose to take the matter up on any such soldierly principle, to do your commerce, and your feeding of nations, for fixed salaries; and to be as particular about giving people the best food, and the best cloth, as soldiers are about giving them the best gunpowder, I could carve something for you on your exchange worth looking at. But I can only at present suggest decorating its frieze with pendant purses; and making its pillars broad at the base for the sticking of bills. And in the innermost chambers of it there might be a statue of Britannia of the Market, who may have, perhaps advisably, a partridge for her crest, typical at once of her courage in fighting for noble ideas; and of her interest in game; and round its neck the inscription in golden letters, "Perdix fovit quæ non peperit."* Then, for her spear, she might have a weaver's beam; and on her shield, instead of her Cross, the Milanese boar, semi-fleeced, with the town of Gennesaret proper in the field, and the legend "In the best market," and her corslet, of leather, folded over her heart in the shape of a purse, with thirty slits in it for a piece of money to go in at, on each day of the month. And I doubt not but that people would come to see your exchange, and its goddess, with applause.

Nevertheless, I want to point out to you certain strange characters in this goddess of yours. She differs from the great Greek and Mediæval deities essentially in two things —first, as to the continuance of her presumed power; secondly, as to the extent of it.

First, as to the Continuance.

The Greek Goddess of Wisdom gave continual increase of wisdom, as the Christian Spirit of Comfort (or Comforter) continual increase of comfort. There was no question, with these, of any limit or cessation of function. But with your Agora Goddess, that is just the most important question. Getting on—but where to? Gathering together —but how much? Do you mean to gather always—never to spend? If so, I wish you joy of your goddess, for I am just as well off as you, without the trouble of worshiping her at all. But if you do not spend, somebody else will— somebody else must. And it is because of this (among many other such errors) that I have fearlessly declared your so-called science of Political Economy to be no

---

* Jerem. xvii. 11 (best in Septuagint and Vulgate). "As the partridge, fostering what she brought not forth, so he that getteth riches, not by right, shall leave them in the midst of his days, and at his end shall be a fool."

science; because, namely, it has omitted the study of exactly the most important branch of the business—the study of *spending*. For spend you must, and as much as you make, ultimately. You gather corn :—will you bury England under a heap of grain; or will you, when you have gathered, finally eat? You gather gold :—will you make your house-roofs of it, or pave your streets with it? That is still one way of spending it. But if you keep it, that you may get more, I'll give you more; I'll give you all the gold you want—all you can imagine—if you can tell me what you'll do with it. You shall have thousands of gold pieces ;—thousands of thousands—millions—mountains, of gold: where will you keep them? Will you put an Olympus of silver upon a golden Pelion—make Ossa like a wart? Do you think the rain and dew would then come down to you, in the streams from such mountains, more blessedly than they will down the mountains which God has made for you, of moss and whinstone? But it is not gold that you want to gather! What is it? greenbacks? No; not those neither. What is it then—is it ciphers after a capital I? Cannot you practice writing ciphers, and write as many as you want? Write ciphers for an hour every morning, in a big book, and say every evening, I am worth all those noughts more than I was yesterday. Won't that do? Well, what in the name of Plutus is it you want? Not gold, not greenbacks, not ciphers after a capital I? You will have to answer, after all, "No; we want, somehow or other, money's *worth*." Well, what is that? Let your Goddess of Getting-on discover it, and let her learn to stay therein.

II. But there is yet another question to be asked respecting this Goddess of Getting-on. The first was of the continuance of her power; the second is of its extent.

Pallas and the Madonna were supposed to be all the world's Pallas, and all the world's Madonna. They could teach all men, and they could comfort all men. But, look strictly into the nature of the power of your Goddess of Getting-on; and you will find she is the Goddess—not of everybody's getting on—but only of somebody's getting on. This is a vital, or rather deathful, distinction. Examine it in your own ideal of the state of national life which this Goddess is to evoke and maintain. I asked you what it was, when I was last here;*—you have never told me. Now, shall I try to tell you?

Your ideal of human life then is, I think, that it should be passed in a pleasant undulating world, with iron and coal everywhere underneath it. On each pleasant bank of this world is to be a beautiful mansion, with two wings; and stables, and coach-houses; a moderately sized park; a large garden and hot houses; and pleasant carriage drives through the shrubberies. In this mansion are to live the favored votaries of the Goddess; the English gentleman, with his gracious wife, and his beautiful family; always able to have the boudoir and the jewels for the wife, and the beautiful ball dresses for the daughters, and hunters for the sons, and a shooting in the Highlands for himself. At the bottom of the bank, is to be the mill; not less than a quarter of a mile long, with a steam engine at each end, and two in the middle, and a chimney three hundred feet high. In this mill are to be in constant employment from eight hundred to a thousand workers, who never drink, never strike, always go to church on Sunday, and always express themselves in respectful language.

Is not that, broadly, and in the main features, the kind of thing you propose to yourselves? It is very pretty indeed

---

* *Two Paths.*

seen from above; not at all so pretty, seen from below. For, observe, while to one family this deity is indeed the Goddess of Getting-on, to a thousand families she is the Goddess of *not* Getting-on. "Nay," you say, "they have all their chance." Yes, so has every one in a lottery, but there must always be the same number of blanks. "Ah! but in a lottery it is not skill and intelligence which take the lead, but blind chance." What then! do you think the old practice, that "they should take who have the power, and they should keep who can," is less iniquitous, when the power has become power of brains instead of fist? and that, though we may not take advantage of a child's or a woman's weakness, we may of a man's foolishness? "Nay, but finally, work must be done, and some one must be at the top, some one at the bottom." Granted, my friends. Work must always be, and captains of work must always be; and if you in the least remember the tone of any of my writings, you must know that they are thought unfit for this age, because they are always insisting on need of government, and speaking with scorn of liberty. But I beg you to observe that there is a wide difference between being captains or governors of work, and taking the profits of it. It does not follow, because you are general of an army, that you are to take all the treasure, or land, it wins (if it fight for treasure or land); neither, because you are king of a nation, that you are to consume all the profits of the nation's work. Real kings, on the contrary, are known invariably by their doing quite the reverse of this,— by their taking the least possible quantity of the nation's work for themselves. There is no test of real kinghood so infallible as that. Does the crowned creature live simply, bravely, unostentatiously? probably he *is* a King. Does he cover his body with jewels, and his table with delicates?

in all probability he is *not* a King. It is possible he may be, as Solomon was; but that is when the nation shares his splendor with him. Solomon made gold, not only to be in his own palace as stones, but to be in Jerusalem as stones. But even so, for the most part, these splendid kinghoods expire in ruin, and only the true kinghoods live, which are of royal laborers governing loyal laborers; who, both leading rough lives, establish the true dynasties. Conclusively you will find that because you are king of a nation, it does not follow that you are to gather for yourself all the wealth of that nation; neither, because you are king of a small part of the nation, and lord over the means of its maintenance—over field, or mill, or mine, are you to take all the produce of that piece of the foundation of national existence for yourself.

You will tell me I need not preach against these things, for I cannot mend them. No, good friends, I cannot; but you can, and you will; or something else can and will. Do you think these phenomena are to stay always in their present power or aspect? All history shows, on the contrary, that to be the exact thing they never can do. Change *must* come; but it is ours to determine whether change of growth, or change of death. Shall the Parthenon be in ruins on its rock, and Bolton priory in its meadow, but these mills of yours be the consummation of the buildings of the earth, and their wheels be as the wheels of eternity? Think you that "men may come, and men may go," but —mills—go on forever? Not so; out of these better or worse shall come; and it is for you to choose which.

I know that none of this wrong is done with deliberate purpose. I know, on the contrary, that you wish your workmen well; that you do much for them, and that you desire to do more for them, if you saw your way to it safely. I know that many of you have done, and are every day doing, whatever you feel to be in your power; and that even all this wrong and misery are brought about by a warped sense of duty, each of you striving to do his best, without noticing that this best is essentially and centrally the best for himself, not for others. And all this has come of the spreading of that thrice accursed, thrice impious doctrine of the modern economist, that "To do the best for yourself, is finally to do the best for others." Friends, our great Master said not so; and most absolutely we shall find this world is not made so. Indeed, to do the best for others, is finally to do the best for ourselves; but it will not do to have our eyes fixed on that issue. The Pagans had got beyond that. Hear what a Pagan says of this matter; hear what were, perhaps, the last written words of Plato,—if not the last actually written (for this we cannot know), yet assuredly in fact and power his parting words— in which, endeavoring to give full crowning and harmonious close to all his thoughts, and to speak the sum of them by the imagined sentence of the Great Spirit, his strength and his heart fail him, and the words cease, broken off for ever. It is the close of the dialogue called "Critias," in which he describes, partly from real tradition, partly in ideal dream, the early state of Athens; and the genesis, and order, and religion, of the fabled isle of Atlantis; in which genesis he conceives the same first perfection and final degeneracy of man, which in our own Scriptural tradition is expressed by saying that the Sons of God intermarried with the daughters of men, for he supposes the earliest race to have been indeed the children of God; and to have corrupted themselves, until "their spot was not the spot of his children." And this, he says, was the end; that indeed "through many generations, so long as the God's nature in them yet was full, they were submissive to the sacred laws, and carried themselves lovingly to all that had kindred with them in divineness; for their uttermost spirit was faithful and true, and in every wise great; so that, in all meakness of wisdom, they dealt with each other, and took all the chances of life; and despising all things except virtue, they cared little what happened day by day, and *bore lightly the burden* of gold and of possessions; for they saw that, if only their common love and virtue increased, all these things would be increased together with them; but to set their esteem and ardent pursuit upon material possession would be to lose that first, and their virtue and affection together with it. And by such reasoning, and what of the divine nature remained in them, they gained all this greatness of which we have already told; but when the God's part of them faded and became extinct, being mixed again and again, and effaced by the prevalent mortality; and the human nature at last exceeded, they then became unable to endure the courses of fortune; and fell into shapelessness of life, and baseness in the sight of him who could see, having lost everything that was fairest of their honor; while to the blind hearts which could not discern the true life, tending to happiness, it seemed that they were then chiefly noble and happy, being filled with all iniquity of inordinate possession and power. Whereupon, the God of Gods, whose Kinghood is in laws, beholding a once just nation thus cast into misery, and desiring to lay such punishment upon them as might make them repent into restraining, gathered together all the gods into his dwelling-place, which from heaven's center overlooks whatever has part in creation; and having assembled them he said''——

The rest is silence. So ended are the last words of the chief wisdom of the heathen, spoken of this idol of riches;

this idol of yours; this golden image high by measureless cubits, set up where your green fields of England are furnace-burnt into the likeness of the plain of Dura: this idol, forbidden to us, first of all idols, by our own Master and faith; forbidden to us also by every human lip that has ever, in any age or people, been accounted of as able to speak according to the purposes of God. Continue to make that forbidden deity your principal one, and soon no more art, no more science, no more pleasure will be possible. Catastrophe will come; or worse than catastrophe, slow moldering and withering into Hades. But if you can fix some conception of a true human state of life to be striven for—life for all men as for yourselves—if you can determine some honest and simple order of existence; following those trodden ways of wisdom, which are pleasantness, and seeking her quiet and withdrawn paths, which are peace;—then, and so sanctifying wealth into "commonwealth," all your art, your literature, your daily labors, your domestic affection, and citizen's duty, will join and increase into one magnificent harmony. You will know then how to build, well enough; you will build with stone well, but with flesh better; temples not made with hands, but riveted of hearts; and that kind of marble, crimson-veined, is indeed eternal.

BOOK III.

SELECTIONS FROM
"FORS CLAVIGERA."

OR

LETTERS TO THE WORKINGMEN AND LABORERS

OF GREAT BRITAIN.

EDITOR'S PREFACE.

FORS CLAVIGERA contains at once the wittiest, the most characteristic, the most radical, and also some of the most exalted and religious writings of John Ruskin. The book, be it remembered, is not an essay, but a collection of letters written at stated times by their author to the workingmen of Great Britain. They are, therefore, what all letters ought to be, unfettered expressions of the writer's feelings, and thoughts, and mood at the time of writing. They show John Ruskin as he is or at least as he was when he wrote them. They give his passing thoughts, speaking now of a Yorkshire pudding, now of a Venetian ferry, now of a reading from Scott, now of a picture by Carpaccio, now of a newspaper clipping, now of a bit of Plato, now of a Hebrew Psalm, now of Tinteretto; yet through it all runs deepest thought and most earnest spirit as to the true conception of society and the duty of living men and women in this actual modern world. No one can read these letters without having many and many a new thought suggested, many and many a new purpose conceived in his heart. No one knows John Ruskin who has not read these letters.

The meaning of the name no one but the author himself can explain. We quote his own words from the second letter. "You may like to know, and ought to know, what I mean by the title of these Letters; and why it is in Latin. I can only tell you in part, for the letters will be on many things, if I am able to carry out my plan in them; and that title means many things, and is in Latin, because I could not have given an English one that meant so many. We, indeed, were not till lately a loquacious people, nor a useless one; but the Romans did more, and said less, than any other nation that ever lived; and their language is the most heroic ever spoken by men.

"Therefore I wish you to know, at least, some words of it, and to recognize what thoughts they stand for.

"Some day, I hope you may know—and that European workmen may know—many words of it; but even a few will be useful..

"Do not smile at my saying so. Of Arithmetic, Geometry, and Chemistry, you can know but little, at the utmost; but that little, well learned, serves you well. And a little Latin, well learned, will serve you also, and in a higher way than any of these.

"'Fors' is the best part of three good English words, Force, Fortitude, and Fortune. I wish you to know the meaning of those three words accurately.

"'Force,' (in humanity), means power of doing good work. A fool, or a corpse, can do any quantity of mischief; but only a wise and strong man, or, with what true vital force there is in him, a weak one, can do good.

"'Fortitude' means the power of bearing necessary pain, or trial of patience, whether by time, or temptation.

"'Fortune' means the necessary fate of a man: the ordinance of his life which cannot be changed. To 'make your Fortune' is to rule that appointed fate to the best ends of which it is capable.

"Fors is a feminine word; and Clavigera is, therefore, the feminine of 'Claviger.'

"Clava means a club. Clavis, a key. Clavus, a nail, or a rudder.

"Gero means 'I carry.' It is the root of our word 'gesture' (the way you carry yourself); and, in a curious by-way, of 'jest.'

"Clavigera may mean, therefore, either Club-bearer, Key-bearer, or Nail-bearer.

"Each of these three possible meanings of Clavigera corresponds to one of the three meanings of Fors.

"Fors, the Club-bearer, means the strength of Hercules or of Deed.

"Fors, the Key-bearer, means the strength of Ulysses, or of Patience.

"Fors, the Nail-bearer, means the strength of Lycurgus, or of Law.

"I will tell you what you may usefully know of those three Greek persons in a little time. At present, note only of the three powers: 1. That the strength of Hercules is for deed, not misdeed; and that his club—the favorite weapon, also, of the Athenian hero Theseus, whose form is the best inheritance left to us by the greatest of Greek sculptors, (it is in the Elgin room of the British Museum, and I shall have much to tell you of him—especially how he helped Hercules in his utmost need, and how he invented mixed vegetable soup)—was for subduing monsters and cruel persons, and was of olive-wood. 2. That the Second Fors Clavigera is portress at a gate which she cannot open till you have waited long; and that her robe is of the color of ashes, or dry earth. 3. That the Third Fors Clavigera, the power of Lycurgus, is Royal as well as Legal; and that the notablest crown yet existing in Europe of any that have been worn by Christian kings, was—people say—made of a Nail.

"That is enough about my title, for this time; now to our work."

We are able in this little volume only to quote a few of the more striking and suggestive passages. We have done so, placing the subject at the head of each selection. On three subjects only we have made selections of some little length: Interest, The St. George's Company, and the Summary of the Teachings of the whole book. The first is important because it strikes the key-note to all of Ruskin's social views, the substitution of a life of honest work, for a life of dishonest income from investment; the second shows how Ruskin thinks it best and most practical to carry out this view of life; the third gives us the whole of *Fors Clavigera* in a nutshell, a most fitting ending to our collection of Ruskin's thoughts on Social Problems.

—ED.

SELECTIONS FROM
FORS CLAVIGERA.

I.—COMMUNISM.

FOR, indeed, I am myself a Communist of the old school—reddest also of the red; and was on the very point of saying so at the end of my last letter; only the telegram about the Louvre's being on fire stopped me, because I thought the Communists of the new school, as I could not at all understand them, might not quite understand me. For we Communists of the old school think that our property belongs to everybody; and everybody's property to us; so of course I thought the Louvre belonged to me as much as to the Parisians, and expected they would have sent word over to me, being an Art Professor, to ask whether I wanted it burnt down. But no message or intimation to that effect ever reached me. . . . .

And this is the last I will tell you for the present, of my new ideas, but a troublesome one: namely, that we are henceforward to have a duplicate power of political economy; and that the new Parisian expression for its first principle is not to be "laissez faire," but "laissez *re*-faire."

I cannot, however, make anything of these new French fashions of thought till I have looked at them quietly a little.

So to-day I will content myself with telling you what we Communists of the old school meant by Communism; and it will be worth your hearing, for—I tell you simply in my "arrogant" way—we know, and have known, what Communism is—for our fathers knew it and told us, three thousand years ago; while you baby Communists do not so much as know what the name means, in your own English or French—no, not so much as whether a House of Commons implies, or does not imply, also a House of Uncommons; nor whether the Holiness of the Commúne, which Garibaldi came to fight for, had any relation to the Holiness of the "Communion" which he came to fight against.

Will you be at the pains, now, however, to learn rightly, and once for all, what Communism is? First, it means that everybody must work in common, and do common or simple work for his dinner; and that if any man will not do it, he must not have his dinner. That much, perhaps, you thought you knew?—but you did not think we Communists of the old school knew it also? You shall have it, then, in the words of the Chelsea farmer and stout Catholic, I was telling you of in our last number. He was born in Milk Street, London, three hundred and ninety-one years ago, and he planned a Commune flowing with milk and honey, and otherwise Elysian; and he called it the "Place of Wellbeing," or Utopia; which is a word you perhaps have occasionally used before now, like others, without understanding it;—(in the article of the Liverpool *Daily Post* before referred to, it occurs felicitously seven times). You shall use it in that stupid way no more, if I can help it. Listen how matters really are managed there.

The chief, and almost the only business of the government, is to take care that no man may live idle, but that every one may follow his trade diligently: yet they do not wear themselves out with perpetual toil from morning to night, as if they were beasts of burden, which, as it is indeed a heavy slavery, so it is everywhere the common course of life amongst all mechanics except the Utopians: but they, dividing the day and night into twenty-four hours, appoint six of these for work, three of which are before dinner and three after; they then sup, and, at eight o'clock, counting from noon, go to bed and sleep eight hours; the rest of their time, besides that taken up in work, eating, and sleeping, is left to every man's discretion; yet they are not to abuse that interval of luxury and idleness, but must employ it in some proper exercise, according to their various inclinations, which is, for the most part, reading.

"But the time appointed for labor is to be narrowly examined, otherwise, you may imagine that, since there are only six hours appointed for work, they may fall under a scarcity of necessary provisions: but it is so far from being true that this time is not sufficient for supplying them with plenty of all things, either necessary or convenient, that it is rather too much; and this you will easily apprehend if you consider how great a part of all other nations is quite idle."

"First, women generally do little, who are the half of mankind; and, if some few women are diligent, their husbands are idle: then,"— . . . .

We will stop a minute, friends, if you please, for I want you, before you read further, to be once more made fully aware that this farmer who is speaking to you is one of the sternest Roman Catholics of his stern time; and, at the fall of Cardinal Wolsey, became Lord High Chancellor of England in his stead.

"—then, consider the great company of idle priests, and

of those that are called religious men; add to these, all rich men, chiefly those who have estates in land, who are called noblemen and gentlemen, together with their families, made up of idle persons, that are kept more for show than use: add to these, all those strong and lusty beggars that go about, pretending some disease in excuse for their begging; and, upon the whole account, you will find, that the number of those by whose labors mankind is supplied is much less than you, perhaps, imagined: then, consider how few of those that work are employed in labors that are of real service! for we, who measure all things by money, give rise to many trades that are both vain and superfluous, and serve only to support riot and luxury: for if those who work were employed only in such things as the conveniences of life require, there would be such an abundance of them, *that the prices of them would so sink that tradesmen could not be maintained by their gains;"*—(italics mine—Fair and softly, Sir Thomas! we must have a shop round the corner, and a pedlar or two on fair-days, yet)—"if all those who labor about useless things were set to more profitable employments, and if all that languish out their lives in sloth and idleness (every one of whom consumes as much as any two of the men that are at work) were forced to labor, you may easily imagine that a small proportion of time would serve for doing all that is either necessary, profitable or pleasant to mankind, especially while pleasure is kept within its due bounds."

So much for the first law of old Communism, respecting work. Then the second respects property, and it is that the public, or common, wealth, shall be more and statelier in all its substance than private or singular wealth; that is to say (to come to my own special business for a moment) that there shall be only cheap and few pictures if any, in the insides of houses, where nobody but the owner can see them; but costly pictures, and many, on the outsides of houses, where the people can see them: also that the Hotel-de-Ville, or Hotel of the whole Town, for the transaction of its common business, shall be a magnificent building, much rejoiced in by the people, and with its tower seen far away through the clear air; but that the hotels for private business or pleasure, cafés, taverns, and the like shall be low, few, plain, and in back streets; more especially such as furnish singular and uncommon drinks and refreshments; but that the fountains that furnish the people's common drink should be very lovely and stately, and adorned with precious marbles, and the like. Then further, according to old Communism, the private dwellings of uncommon persons—dukes and lords—are to be very simple, and roughly put together—such persons being supposed to be above all care for things that please the commonalty; but the buildings for public or common service, more especially schools, almshouses and workhouses, are to be externally of a majestic character, as being for noble purposes and charities; and in their interiors furnished with many luxuries for the poor and sick. And finally and chiefly, it is an absolute law of old Communism that the fortunes of private persons should be small, and of little account in the State; but the common treasure of the whole nation should be of superb and precious things in redundant quantity, as pictures, statues, precious books; gold and silver vessels, preserved from ancient times; gold and silver bullion laid up for use, in case of any chance need of buying anything suddenly from foreign nations; noble horses, cattle and sheep, on the public lands; and vast spaces of land for culture, exercise, and garden, round the cities, full of flowers, which, being everybody's property, nobody could gather; and of birds, which, being everybody's property, nobody could shoot. And, in a word, that instead of a common poverty, or national debt, which every poor person in the nation is taxed annually to fulfill his part of, there should be a common wealth, or national reverse of debt, consisting of pleasant things, which every poor person in the nation should be summoned to receive his dole of, annually; and of pretty things, which every person capable of admiration, foreigners as well as natives, should unfeignedly admire, in an æsthetic, and not a covetous, manner (though for my own part, I can't understand what it is that I am taxed now to defend, or what foreign nations are supposed to covet, here). But truly, a nation that has got anything to defend of real public interest, can usually hold it; and a fat Latin communist gave for sign of the strength of his commonalty, in its strongest time,—

> "Privatus illis census erat brevis,
> Commune magnum."

II.—FREEDOM OR SLAVERY.

FREEMEN, indeed! You are slaves, not to masters of any strength or honor; but to the idlest talkers at that floral end of Westminster bridge. Nay, to countless meaner masters than they. For though, indeed, as early as the year 1102, it was decreed in a council at St. Peter's, Westminster, "that no man for the future should presume to carry on the wicked trade of selling men in the markets, like brute beasts, which hitherto had been the common custom of England," the no less wicked trade of *under*-selling men in markets has lasted to this day; producing conditions of slavery differing from the ancient ones only in being starved instead of full-fed: and besides this, a state of slavery unheard of among the nations till now, has arisen with us. In all former slaveries, Egyptian, Algerine, Saxon, and American, the slave's complaint has been of compulsory *work*. But the modern Politico-Economic slave is a new and far more injured species, condemned to Compulsory *Idleness*, for fear he should spoil other people's trade; the beautifully logical condition of the national Theory of Economy in this matter being that, if you are a shoemaker, it is a law of Heaven that you must sell your goods under their price, in order to destroy the trade of other shoemakers; but if you are not a shoemaker, and are going shoeless and lame, it is a law of Heaven that you must not cut yourself a bit of cowhide, to put between your foot and the stones, because that would interfere with the total trade of shoemaking.

Which theory, of all the wonderful—!

* * * * *

III.—MACHINERY.

YOU think it a great triumph to make the sun draw brown landscapes for you. That was also a discovery and some day may be useful. But the sun had drawn landscapes before for you, not in brown, but in green, and blue, and all imaginable colors, here in England. Not one of you ever looked at them then; not one of you cares for the loss of them now, when you have shut the sun out with smoke, so that he can draw nothing more, except brown blots through a hole in a box. There was a rocky valley between Buxton and Bakewell, once upon a time, divine as the Vale of Tempe; you might have seen the Gods there morning and evening—Apollo and all the sweet Muses of the Light—walking in fair procession on the lawns of it, and to and fro among the pinnacles of its crags. You cared neither for Gods nor grass, but for cash (which you did not know the way to get); you thought you could get it by what the *Times* calls "Railroad Enterprise." You Enterprised a Railroad through the valley—you blasted its rocks away, heaped thousands of tons of shale into its lovely stream. The valley is gone, and the Gods with it; and now, every fool in Buxton can be at Bakewell in half an hour, and every fool in Bakewell at Buxton; which you think a lucrative process of exchange—you Fools Everywhere.

Observe. A man and a woman, with their children, properly trained, are able easily to cultivate as much ground as will feed them; to build as much wall and roof as will lodge them, and to spin and weave as much cloth as will clothe them. They can all be perfectly happy and healthy in doing this. Supposing that they invent machinery which will build, plow, thresh, cook, and weave, and that they have none of these things any more to do, but may read, or cricket, all day long, I believe myself that they will neither be so good nor so happy as without the machines. But I waive my belief in this matter for the time. I will assume that they become more refined and moral persons, and that idleness is in future to be the mother of all good. But observe, I repeat, the power of your machine is only in enabling them to be idle. It will not enable them to live better than they did before, nor to live in greater numbers. Get your heads quite clear on this matter. Out of so much ground, only so much living is to be got, with or without machinery. You may set a million of steam-plows to work on an acre, if you like— out of that acre only a given number of grains of corn will grow, scratch or scorch it as you will. So that the question is not at all whether, by having more machines, more of you can live. No machines will increase the possibilities of life. They only increase the possibilities of idleness. Suppose, for instance, you could get the oxen in your plow driven by a goblin, who would ask for no pay, not even a cream bowl,—(you have nearly managed to get it driven by an iron goblin, as it is;)—Well, your furrow will take no more seeds than if you had held the stilts yourself. But, instead of holding them, you sit, I presume, on a bank beside the field, under an eglantine;—watch the goblin at its work, and read poetry. Meantime, your wife in the house has also got a goblin to weave and wash for her. And she is lying on the sofa, reading poetry.

IV.—TAXES.

DO you see, in *The Times* of yesterday and the day before, 22nd and 23rd June, that the Minister of France dares not, even in this her utmost need, put on an income tax ; and do you see why he dares not?

Observe, such a tax is the only honest and just one; because it tells on the rich in true proportion to the poor, and because it meets necessity in the shortest and bravest way, and without interfering with any commercial operation.

All rich people object to income tax, of course;—they like to pay as much as a poor man pays on their tea, sugar, and tobacco—nothing on their incomes.

Whereas, in true justice, the only honest and wholly right tax is one not merely on income, but property; increasing in percentage as the property is greater. And the main virtue of such a tax is that it makes publicly known what every man has, and how he gets it.

For every kind of Vagabonds, high and low, agree in their dislike to give an account of the way they get their living, still less, of how much they have got sewn up in their breeches. It does not, however, matter much to a country that it should know how its poor Vagabonds live; but it is of vital moment that it should know how its rich Vagabonds live; and that much of knowledge, it seems to me, in the present state of our education, is quite attainable. But that, when you have attained it, you may act on it wisely, the first need is that you should be sure you are living honestly yourselves. That is why I told you in my second letter, you must learn to obey good laws before you seek to alter bad ones:—I will amplify now a little the three promises I want you to make. Look back at them.

I. You are to do good work, whether you live or die. It may be you will have to die;—well, men have died for their country often, yet doing her no good; be ready to die for her in doing her assured good: her, and all other countries with her. Mind your own business with your absolute heart and soul; but see that it is a good business first. That it *is* corn and sweet peas you are producing, —not gunpowder and arsenic. And be sure of this, literally:—*you must simply rather die than make any destroying mechanism or compound*. You are to be *literally* employed in cultivating the ground, or making useful things, and carrying them where they are wanted. Stand in the streets, and say to all who pass by:—Have you any vineyard we can work in,—*not* Naboth's? In your powder and petroleum manufactory we work no more.

I have said little to you yet of any of the pictures engraved—you perhaps think, not to the ornament of my book.

Be it so. You will find them better than ornaments in time. Notice, however, in the one I give you with this letter—the "Charity" of Giotto—the Red Queen of Dante, and ours also,—how different his thought of her is from the common one.

Usually she is nursing children, or giving money. Giotto thinks there is little charity in nursing children;— bears and wolves do that for their little ones; and less still in giving money.

His Charity tramples upon bags of Gold—has no use for them. She gives only corn and flowers; and God's angel gives *her*, not even these—but a Heart.

Giotto is quite literal in his meaning, as well as figurative. Your love is to give food and flowers, and to labor for them only.

But what are we to do against powder and petroleum, then? What men may do; not what poisonous beasts may. If a wretch spits in your face, will you answer by spitting in his? if he throw vitriol at you, will you go to the apothecary for a bigger bottle?

There is no physical crime, at this day, so far beyond pardon,—so without parallel in its untempted guilt, as the making of war-machinery, and invention of mischievous substance. Two nations may go mad, and fight like harlots —God have mercy on them ;—you, who hand them carving-knives off the table, for leave to pick up a dropped sixpence, what mercy is there for *you* ? We are so humane, forsooth, and so wise; and our ancestors had tar-barrels for witches; *we* will have them for everybody else, and drive the witches' trade ourselves, by daylight; we will have our cauldrons, please Hecate, cooled (according to the Darwinian theory), with baboons' blood, and enough of it, and sell hell-fire in the open streets.

II. Seek to revenge no injury. You see now—do not you—a little more clearly why I wrote that? what strain there is on the untaught masses of you to revenge themselves, even with insane fire?

Alas, the Taught masses are strained enough also;— have you not just seen a great religious and reformed nation, with its goodly Captains—philosophical,—sentimental,—domestic,—evangelical-angelical-minded altogether, and with its Lord's Prayer really quite vital to it,—come and take its neighbor nation by the throat, saying, "Pay me that thou owest."

Seek to revenge no injury: I do not say, seek to punish no crime: look what I hinted about failed bankers. Of that hereafter.

III. Learn to obey good laws; and in a little while, you will reach the better learning—how to obey good Men, who are living, breathing, unblinded law; and to subdue base and disloyal ones, recognizing in those the light, and ruling over these the power, of the Lord of Light and Peace, whose Dominion is an everlasting Dominion, and his Kingdom from generation to generation.

V.—CLERGYMEN.

I HAD an impatient remonstrance sent me the other day, by a country clergyman's wife, against that saying in my former letter, "Dying has been more expensive to you than living." Did I know, she asked, what a country clergyman's life was, and that he was the poor man's only friend.

Alas, I know it, and too well. What can be said of more deadly and ghastly blame against the clergy of England, or any other country, than that they are the poor man's only friends?

Have they, then, so betrayed their Master's charge and mind, in their preaching to the rich;—so smoothed their words, and so sold their authority,—that, after twelve hundred years entrusting of the gospel to them, there is no man in England (this is their chief plea for themselves forsooth) who will have mercy on the poor, but they; and so they must leave the word of God, and serve tables?

I would not myself have said so much against English clergymen, whether of country or town. Three—and one dead makes four—of my dear friends (and I have not many dear friends) are country clergymen; and I know the ways of every sort of them; my architectural tastes necessarily bringing me into near relations with the sort who like pointed arches and painted glass; and my old religious breeding having given me an unconquerable habit of taking up with any traveling tinker of evangelical principles I may come across; and even of reading, not without awe, the prophetic warnings of any persons belonging to that peculiarly well-informed "persuasion," such, for instance, as those of Mr. Zion Ward "Concerning the fall of Lucifer, in a letter to a friend, Mr. William Dick, of Glasgow, price twopence," in which I read (as aforesaid, with unfeigned feelings of concern), that "the slain of the Lord shall be MAN-Y; that is, man, in whom death is, with all the works of carnality, shall be burned up!"

But I was not thinking either of English clergy, or of any other group of clergy, specially, when I wrote that sentence; but of the entire Clerkly or Learned Company, from the first priest of Egypt to the last ordained Belgravian curate, and of all the talk they have talked, and all the quarreling they have caused, and all the gold they have had given them, to this day, when still, "they are the poor man's only friends"—and by no means all of them that, heartily! though I see the Bishop of Manchester has of late been superintending—I beg his pardon, Bishops don't superintend—looking on, or over, I should have said,—the recreations of his flock at the seaside; and "the thought struck him" that railroads were an advantage to them in taking them for their holiday out of Manchester. The thought may, perhaps, strike him, next, that a working man ought to be able to find "holy days" *in* his home, as well as out of it.*

A year or two ago, a man who had at the time, and has still, important official authority over much of the business of the country, was speaking anxiously to me of the misery increasing in the suburbs and back streets of London, and debating, with the good help of the Oxford Regius Professor of Medicine—who was second in council—what

---

* See § 159, (written seven years ago), in *Munera Pulveris.*

sanitary or moral remedy could be found. The debate languished, however, because of the strong conviction in the minds of all three of us that the misery was inevitable in the suburbs of so vast a city. At last, either the minister or physician, I forget which, expressed the conviction. "Well," I answered, "then you must not have large cities." "That," answered the minister, "is an unpractical saying—you know we *must* have them, under existing circumstances."

I made no reply, feeling that it was vain to assure any man actively concerned in modern parliamentary business, that no measures were "practical" except those which touched the source of the evil opposed.

VI.—CARLYLE.

READ your Carlyle, then, with all your heart, and with the best of brain you can give; and you will learn from him first, the eternity of good law, and the need of obedience to it: then, concerning your own immediate business, you will learn further this, that the beginning of all good law, and nearly the end of it, is in these two ordinances,—That every man shall do good work for his bread; and secondly, That every man shall have good bread for his work. But the first of these is the only one you have to think of. If you are resolved that the work shall be good, the bread will be sure; if not,—believe me, there is neither steam plow nor steam mill, go they never so glibly, that will win it from the earth long, either for you, or the Ideal Landed Proprietor.

VII.—EXPECTANTS OF TURNIPS.

VIRTUALLY, the entire business of the world turns on the clear necessity of getting on table, hot or cold, if possible, meat—but, at least, vegetables,—at some hour of the day, for all of us: for you laborers, we will say at noon; for us æsthetical persons, we will say at eight in the evening; for we like to have done our eight hours' work of admiring abbeys before we dine. But, at some time of day, the mutton and turnips, or, since mutton itself is only a transformed state of turnips, we may say, as sufficiently typical of everything, turnips only, must absolutely be got for us both. And nearly every problem of State policy and economy, as at present understood, and practiced, consists in some device for persuading you laborers to go and dig up dinner for us reflective and æsthetical persons, who like to sit still, and think, or admire. So that when we get to the bottom of the matter, we find the inhabitants of this earth broadly divided into two great masses;—the peasant paymasters—spade in hand, original and imperial producers of turnips; and, waiting on them all round, a crowd of polite persons, modestly expectant of turnips, for some—too often theoretical—service.

VIII.—RICH?

I HAD to go to Verona by the afternoon train. In the carriage with me were two American girls with their father and mother, people of the class which has lately made so much money suddenly, and does not know what to do with it: and these two girls, of about fifteen and eighteen, had evidently been indulged in everything, (since they had had the means,) which western civilization could imagine. And here they were, specimens of the utmost which the money and invention of the nineteenth century could produce in maidenhood,—children of its most progressive race,—enjoying the full advantages of political liberty, of enlightened philosophical education, of cheap pilfered literature, and of luxury at any cost. Whatever money, machinery, or freedom of thought, could do for these two children, had been done. No superstition had deceived, no restraint degraded them :—types, they could not but be, of maidenly wisdom and felicity, as conceived by the forwardest intellects of our time.

And they were traveling through a district which, if any in the world, should touch the hearts and delight the eyes of young girls. Between Venice and Verona ! Portia's villa perhaps in sight upon the Brenta,—Juliet's tomb to be visited in the evening,—blue against the southern sky, the hills of Petrarch's home. Exquisite midsummer sunshine, with low rays, glanced through the vine-leaves ; all the Alps were clear, from the lake of Garda to Cadore, and to furthest Tyrol. What a princess's chamber, this, if these are princesses, and what dreams might they not dream, therein!

But the two American girls were neither princesses, nor seers, nor dreamers. By infinite self-indulgence, they had reduced themselves simply to two pieces of white putty that could feel pain. The flies and dust stuck to them as to clay, and they perceived, between Venice and Verona, nothing but the flies and the dust. They pulled down the blinds the moment they entered the carriage, and then sprawled, and writhed, and tossed among the cushions of it, in vain contest, during the whole fifty miles, with every miserable sensation of bodily affliction that could make time intolerable. They were dressed in thin white frocks, coming vaguely open at the backs as they stretched or wriggled; they had French novels, lemons, and lumps of sugar, to beguile their state with; the novels hanging together by the ends of string that had once stitched them, or adhering at the corners in densely bruised dog's-ears, out of which the girls, wetting their fingers, occasionally extricated a gluey leaf. From time to time they cut a lemon open, ground a lump of sugar backward and forward over it till every fiber was in a treacly pulp; then sucked the pulp, and gnawed the white skin into leathery strings, for the sake of its bitter. Only one sentence was exchanged, in the fifty miles, on the subject of things outside the carriage (the Alps being once visible from a station where they had drawn up the blinds).

"Don't those snow-caps make you cool?"

"No—I wish they did."

And so they went their way, with sealed eyes and tormented limbs. their numbered miles of pain.

IX.—INTEREST.

NOW then for Mr. Fawcett:—At the 146th page of the edition of his Manual previously quoted, you will find it stated that the interest of money consists of three distinct parts:

1. Reward for abstinence.
2. Compensation for the risk of loss.
3. Wages for the labor of superintendence.

I will reverse this order in examining the statements; for the only real question is as to the first, and we had better at once clear the other two away from it.

3. Wages for the labor of superintendence.

By giving the capitalist wages at all, we put him at once into the class of laborers, which in my November letter I showed you is partly right; but, by Mr. Fawcett's definition, and in the broad results of business, he is not a laborer. So far as he is one, of course, like any other, he is to be paid for his work. There is no question but that the partner who superintends any business should be paid for superintendence; but the question before us is only respecting payment for doing nothing. I have, for instance, at this moment £15,000 of bank stock, and receive £1,200 odd, a year, from the Bank, but I have never received the slightest intimation from the directors that they wished for my assistance in the superintendence of that establishment; —(more shame for them). But even in cases where the partners are active, it does not follow that the one who has most money in the business is either fittest to superintend it, or likely to do so; it is indeed probable that a man who has made money already will know how to make more; and it is necessary to attach some importance to property as the sign of sense: but your business is to choose and pay your superintendent for his sense, and not for his money. Which is exactly what Mr. Carlyle has been telling you for some time; and both he and all his disciples entirely approve of interest, if you are indeed prepared to define that term as payment for the exercise of common sense spent in the service of the person who pays for it. I reserve yet awhile, however, what is to be said, as hinted in my first letter, about the sale of ideas.

2. Compensation for risk.

Does Mr. Fawcett mean by compensation for risk, protection from it, or reward for running it? Every business involves a certain quantity of risk, which is properly covered by every prudent merchant, but he does not expect to make a profit out of his risks, nor calculate on a percentage on his insurance. If he prefer not to insure, does Professor Fawcett mean that his customers ought to compensate him for his anxiety; and that while the definition of the first part of interest is extra payment for prudence, the definition of the second part of interest is extra payment for *im*prudence? Or, does Professor Fawcett mean, what is indeed often the fact, that interest for money represents such reward for risk as people may get across the green cloth at Homburg or Monaco? Because so far as what used to be business is, in modern political economy, gambling, Professor Fawcett will please to observe that what one gamester gains another loses. You cannot get anything out of Nature, or from God, by gambling;—only out of your neighbor: and to the quantity of interest of money thus gained, you are mathematically to oppose a precisely equal *dis*interest of somebody else's money.

These second and third reasons for interest then, assigned by Professor Fawcett, have evidently nothing whatever to do with the question. What I want to know is, why the Bank of England is paying me £1,200 a year. It certainly does not pay me for superintendence. And so far from receiving my dividend as compensation for risk, I put my money into the bank because I thought it exactly the safest place to put it in. But nobody can be more anxious than I to find it proper that I should have £1,200 a year. Finding two of Mr. Fawcett's reasons fail me utterly, I cling with tenacity to the third, and hope the best from it.

The third, or first,—and now too sorrowfully the last— of the Professor's reasons, is this, that my £1,200 are given me as "the reward of abstinence." It strikes me, upon this that if I had not my £15,000 of Bank Stock I should be a good deal more abstinent than I am, and that nobody would then talk of rewarding me for it. It might be possible to find even cases of very prolonged and painful abstinence, for which no reward has yet been adjudged by less abstinent England. Abstinence may, indeed, have its reward, nevertheless; but not by increase of what we abstain from, unless there be a law of growth for it, unconnected with our abstinence. "You cannot have your cake and eat it." Of course not; and if you don't eat it, you have your cake; but not a cake and a half! Imagine the complex trial of schoolboy minds, if the law of nature about cakes were, that if you ate none of your cake to-day, you would have ever so much bigger a cake to-morrow!—which is Mr. Fawcett's notion of the law of nature about money; and, alas, many a man's beside,—it being no law of nature whatever, but absolutely contrary to all her laws, and not to be enacted by the whole force of united mankind.

Not a cake and a quarter to-morrow, dunce, however

abstinent you are—only the cake you have,—if the mice don't get at it in the night.

Interest, then, is not, it appears, payment for labor; it is not reward for risk; it is not reward for abstinence.

What is it?

One of two things it is;—taxation, or usury. Of which in my next letter.

An impatient correspondent of mine, Mr. W. C. Sillar, who has long been hotly engaged in testifying publicly against the wickedness of taking interest, writes to me that all I say is mysterious, that I am bound to speak plainly, and above everything, if I think taking interest sinful, not to hold bank stock.

Once for all, then, Mr. Sillar is wholly right as to the abstract fact that lending for gain is sinful; and he has in various pamphlets, shown unanswerably that whatever is said either in the Bible, or in any other good and ancient book, respecting usury, is intended by the writers to apply to the receiving of interest, be it ever so little. But Mr. Sillar has allowed this idea to take possession of him, body and soul; and is just as fondly enthusiastic about abolition of usury as some other people are about the liquor laws. Now of course drunkenness is mischievous, and usury is mischievous, and whoredom is mischievous, and idleness is mischievous. But we cannot reform the world by preaching temperance only, nor refusal of interest only, nor chastity only, nor industry only. I am myself more set on teaching healthful industry than anything else, as the beginning of all redemption; then, purity of heart and body; if I can get these taught, I know that nobody so taught will either get drunk, or, in any unjust manner, "either a borrower or a lender be." But I expect also far higher results than either of these, on which, being utterly bent, I am very careless about such minor matters as the present conditions either of English brewing or banking. I hold bank stock simply because I suppose it to be safer than any other stock, and I take the interest of it, because though taking interest is, in the abstract, as wrong as war, the entire fabric of society is at present so connected with both usury and war, that it is not possible violently to withdraw, nor wisely to set example of withdrawing, from either evil. I entirely, in the abstract, disapprove of war; yet have the profoundest sympathy with Colonel Yea and his fusiliers at Alma, and only wish I had been there with them. I have by no means equal sympathy either with bankers or landlords; but am certain that for the present it is better that I receive my dividends as usual, and that Miss Hill should continue to collect my rents in Marylebone.

"Ananias over again, or worse," Mr. Sillar will probably exclaim, when he reads this, and invoke lightning against me. I will abide the issue of his invocation, and only beg him to observe respecting either ancient or modern denunciations of interest, that they are much beside the mark unless they are accompanied with some explanation of the manner in which borrowing and lending, when necessary, can be carried on without it. Neither *are* often necessary in healthy states of society; but they always must remain so to some extent; and the name "Mount of Pity,"* given

---

* The "Mount" is the heap of money in store for lending without interest. You shall have a picture of it in next number, as drawn by a brave landscape painter four hundred years ago; and it will ultimately be one of the crags of our own Mont Rose; and well should be, for it was first·raised among the rocks of Italy by a Franciscan monk, for refuge to the poor against the usury of the Lombard merchants who gave name to our Lombard Street, and perished by their usury, as their successors are like enough to do also. But the story goes back to Friedrich II. of Germany again, and is too long for this letter.

still in French and Italian to the pawnbroker's shop, descends from a time when lending to the poor was as much a work of mercy as giving to them. And both lending and borrowing are virtuous, when the borrowing is prudent, and the lending kind; how much otherwise than kind lending at interest usually is, you, I suppose, do not need to be told; but how much otherwise than prudent nearly all borrowing is, and above everything, trade on a large scale on borrowed capital, it is very necessary for us all to be told. And for a beginning of other people's words, here are some quoted by Mr. Sillar from a work on the Labor question recently published in Canada, which, though common-place, and evidently the expressions of a person imperfectly educated, are true, earnest, and worth your reading :—

"These Scripture usury laws, then, are for no particular race and for no particular time. They lie at the very foundations of national progress and wealth. They form the only great safeguards of labor, and are the security of civil society, and the strength and protection of commerce itself. Let us beware, for our own sakes, how we lay our hand upon the barriers which God has reared around the humble dwelling of the laboring man. . . . .

"Business itself is a pleasure, but it is the anxieties and burdens of business arising all out of this debt system, which have caused so many aching pillows and so many broken hearts. What countless multitudes, during the last three hundred years, have gone down to bankruptcy and shame—what fair prospects have been forever blighted—what happy homes desolated—what peace destroyed—what ruin and destruction have ever marched hand in hand with this system of debt, paper, and usury! Verily its sins have reached unto heaven, and its iniquities are very great.

"What shall the end of these things be? God only knoweth. I fear the system is beyond a cure. All the great interests of humanity are overborne by it, and nothing can flourish as it ought till it is taken out of the way. It contains within itself, as we have at times witnessed, most potent elements of destruction which in one hour may bring all its riches to nought."

. . . . It may be, that as we fix our laws in further detail, we may add some of the heavier yokes of Lycurgus, or Numa, or John the Baptist: and, though the Son of Man came eating and drinking, and turning water into wine, we may think it needful to try how some of us like living on locusts, or wild honey, or Spartan broth. But at least, I repeat, we are here, in England, to obey the law of Christ, if nothing more.

Now the law of Christ about money and other forms of personal wealth, is taught, first in parables, in which He likens himself to the masters of this world, and explains the conduct which Christians should hold to Him, their heavenly Master, by that which they hold on earth, to earthly ones.

He likens himself, in these stories, several times, to unkind or unjust masters, and especially to hard and usurious ones. And the gist of the parables in each case is, "If ye do so, and are thus faithful to hard and cruel masters, in earthly things, how much more should ye be faithful to a merciful Master, in heavenly things?"

Which argument, evil-minded men wrest, as they do also the other scriptures, to their own destruction. And instead of reading, for instance, in the parable of the Usurer, the intended lesson of industry in the employment of God's gifts, they read in it a justification of the crime which, in other parts of the same scripture, is directly forbidden. And there is indeed no doubt that, if the other prophetic parts of the Bible be true, these stories are so worded that they *may* be touchstones of the heart. They are nets, which sift the kindly reader from the selfish. The parable of the Usurer is like a mill sieve:—the fine flour falls through it, bolted finer; the chaff sticks in it.

Therefore, the only way to understand these difficult parts of the Bible, or even to approach them with safety, is first to read and obey the easy ones. Then the difficult ones all become beautiful and clear :—otherwise they remain venomous enigmas, with a Sphinx of destruction provoking false souls to read them, and ruining them in their own replies.

Now the orders, "not to lay up treasure for ourselves on earth," and to "sell that we have, and give alms," and to "provide ourselves bags which wax not old," are perfectly direct, unmistakable,—universal; and while we are not at all likely to be blamed by God for not imitating Him as a Judge, we shall assuredly be condemned by Him for not, under Judgment, doing as we were bid. But even if we do not feel able to obey these orders, if we must and will lay up treasures on earth, and provide ourselves bags with holes in them,—God may perhaps still, with scorn, permit us in our weakness, provided we are content with our earthly treasures, when we have got them, and don't oppress our brethren, and grind down their souls with them. We may have our old bag about our neck, if we will, and go to heaven like beggars;—but if we sell our brother also, and put the price of his life in the bag, we need not think to enter the kingdom of God so loaded. A rich man may, though hardly, enter the kingdom of heaven without repenting him of his riches; but not the thief, without repenting his theft; nor the adulterer, without repenting his adultery; nor the usurer, without repenting his usury.

The nature of which last sin, let us now clearly understand, once for all.

Mr. Harrison's letter, published in the *Fors* for June, is perhaps no less valuable as an evidence of the subtlety with which this sin has seized upon and paralyzed the public mind (so that even a man of Mr. Harrison's general intelligence has no idea why I ask a question about it), than as a clear statement of the present condition of the law, produced by the usurers who *are* "law-makers" for England, though lawyers are not.

Usury is properly the taking of money for the loan or use of anything (over and above what pays for wear and tear), such use involving no care or labor on the part of the lender. It includes all investments of capital whatsoever, returning "dividends," as distinguished from labor wages, or profits. Thus anybody who works on a railroad as plate-layer, or stoker, has a right to wages for his work; and any inspector of wheels or rails has a right to payment for such inspection; but idle persons who have only paid a hundred pounds toward the road-making, have a right to the return of the hundred pounds,—and no more. If they take a farthing more, they are usurers. They may take fifty pounds for two years, twenty-five for four, five for twenty, or one for a hundred. But the first farthing they take more than their hundred, be it sooner or later, is usury.

Again, when we build a house, and let it, we have a right to as much rent as will return us the wages of our labor, and the sum of our outlay. If, as in ordinary cases, not laboring with our hands or head, we have simply paid say—£1,000—to get the house built, we have a right to the £1,000 back again at once, if we sell it; or, if we let it, to £500 rent during two years, or £100 rent during ten years, or £10 rent during a hundred years. But if, sooner or later, we take a pound more than the thousand, we are usurers.

And thus in all other possible or conceivable cases, the moment our capital is "increased" by having lent it, be it but in the estimation of a hair, that hair's-breadth of increase is usury, just as much as stealing a farthing is theft, no less than stealing a million.

But usury is worse than theft, in so far as it is obtained either by deceiving people, or distressing them; generally by both: and finally by deceiving the usurer himself, who comes to think that usury is a real increase, and that money can grow of money.; whereas all usury is increase to one person only by decrease to another; and every grain of calculated Increment to the Rich, is balanced by its mathematical equivalent of Decrement to the Poor. The Rich have hitherto only counted their gain; but the day is coming, when the Poor will also count their loss—with political results hitherto unparalleled.

For instance, my good old hairdresser at Camberwell came to me the other day, very uncomfortable about his rent. He wanted a pound or two to make it up; and none of his customers wanted their hair cut. I gave him the pound or two,—with the result, I hope my readers have sagacity enough to observe, of distinct decrement to *me*, as increment to the landlord; and then inquired of him, how much he had paid for rent, during his life. On rough calculation, the total sum proved to be between 1,500 and 1,700 pounds. And after paying this sum,—earned, shilling by shilling, with careful snippings, and studiously skillful manipulation of tongs,—here is my poor old friend, now past sixty, practically without a roof over his head;— just as roofless in his old age as he was in the first days of life,—and nervously wandering about Peckham Rye and East Norwood, in the east winter winds, to see if, perchance, any old customers will buy some balm for their thinning locks—and give him the blessed balm of an odd half-crown or two, to rent shelter for his own, for three months more.

Now, supposing that £1,500 of his had been properly laid out, on the edification of lodgings for him, £500 should have built him a serviceable tenement and shop; another £500 have met the necessary repairing expenses for forty years; and at this moment he ought to have had his efficient freehold cottage, with tile and wall right weather-proof, and a nice little nest-egg of five hundred pounds in the Bank, besides. But instead of this, the thousand pounds has gone in payment to slovenly builders, each getting their own percentage, and doing as bad work as possible, under the direction of landlords paying for as little as possible of any sort of work. And the odd five hundred has gone into the landlord's pocket. Pure increment to him; pure decrement to my decoratively laborious friend. No gain "begotten" of money; but simple subtraction from the pocket of the laboring person, and simple addition to the pocket of the idle one.

I have no mind to waste the space of *Fors* in giving variety of instances. Any honest and sensible reader, if he chooses, can think out the truth in such matters for himself. If he be dishonest, or foolish, no one can teach him. If he is resolved to find reason or excuse for things as they are, he may find refuge in one lie after another; and, dislodged from each in turn, fly from the last back to the one he began with. But there will not long be need for debate—nor time for it. Not all the lying lips of commercial Europe can much longer deceive the people in their rapidly increasing distress, nor arrest their straight battle with the cause of it. Through what confused noise and garments rolled in blood,—through what burning and fuel of fire, they will work out their victory,—God only knows, nor what they will do to Barabbas, when they have found out that he *is* a Robber, and not a King. But that discovery of his character and capacity draws very near: and no less change in the world's ways than the former fall of Feudalism itself.

In the meantime, for those of us who are Christians, our own way is plain. We can with perfect ease ascertain what usury is; and in what express terms forbidden. . . . .

"And if thy brother be poor, and powerless with his hands, at thy side, thou shalt take his part upon thee, to help him,* as thy proselyte and thy neighbor; and thy brother shall live with thee. Thou shalt take no usury of him, nor anything over and above, and thou shalt fear thy God. I am the Lord, and thy brother shall live with thee. Thou shalt not give him thy money, for usury; and thou shalt not give him thy food, for increase."

There is the simple law for all of us;—one of those which Christ assuredly came not to destroy, but to fulfill: and there is no national prosperity to be had but in obedience to it.

How we usurers are to live, with the hope of our gains gone, is precisely the old temple of Diana question. How Robin Hood or Cœur de Lion were to live without arrow or axe, would have been as strange a question to *them*, in their day. And there are many amiable persons who will not directly see their way, any more than I do myself, to an honest life; only, let us be sure that this we are leading now is a dishonest one; and worse (if Dante and Shakspeare's mind on the matter are worth any heed, of which more in due time), being neither more nor less than a

---

* Meaning, to do his work instead of him. Compare Acts xx. 35. "I have showed you all things, how that, so laboring, ye ought to *support* the weak."

spiritual manner of cannibalism, which so long as we persist in, every word spoken in Scripture of those who "eat my people as they eat bread," is spoken directly of us.* It may be an encouragement to some of us—especially those evangelically bred—in weaning ourselves slowly from such habits.

X.—ST. GEORGE'S COMPANY.

AS I am now often asked, in private letters, the constitution of St. George's Company, and cannot, hitherto, refer, in answer, to any clear summary of it, I will try to write such a summary in this number of *Fors;* that it may henceforward be sent to inquirers as alone sufficiently explanatory.

The St. George's Company is a society established to carry out certain charitable objects, toward which it invites, and thankfully will receive, help from any persons caring to give it, either in money, labor, or any kind of gift. But

---

* Dear Mr. Ruskin, *8th July*, 1876.
    I see that you intend to speak on the question of usury in next *Fors*. Would it not be well, since the Bishops of the Established Church have not a word to offer in defense of their conduct, to appeal to some of the other sects that profess to take the teaching of the Bible and of Christ for their guidance? The Wesleyans, for instance, teach that the Bible was given almost verbally by the Spirit of God; and John Wesley says his followers are "*to die sooner than put anything in pawn, or borrow and lend on usury.*" Perhaps if you were to challenge the President and Conference, and call on them either to state that they do not accept the teaching of Moses, David, and Christ on this matter, or to bring the sin clearly before the minds of the members of their body, you might force the question on the attention of the professedly religious persons in the country.
                                                         A READER OF FORS.

the Company itself consists of persons who agree in certain general principles of action, and objects of pursuit, and who can, therefore, act together in effective and constant unison.

These objects of pursuit are, in brief terms, the health, wealth, and long life of the British nation: the Company having thus devoted itself, in the conviction that the British nation is at present unhealthy, poor, and likely to perish, as a power, from the face of the earth. They accordingly propose to themselves the general medicining, enriching, and preserving in political strength, of the population of these islands; they themselves numbering at present, in their ranks, about thirty persons,—none of them rich, several of them sick, and the leader of them, at all events, not likely to live long.

Whether the nation be healthy, or in unwholesome degradation of body and mind; wealthy, or in continual and shameful distress; strong, or in rapid decline of political power and authority,—the reader will find debated throughout the various contents of the preceding volumes of *Fors*. But there is one public fact, which cannot be debated—that the nation is in debt. And the St. George's Company do practically make it their *first*, though not their principal, object, to bring *that* state of things to an end; and to establish, instead of a National Debt, a National Store. (See the last line of the fifth page of the first letter of the series, published 1st January, 1871, and the eleventh, and twenty-seventh, letters, throughout.)

That very few readers of *this* page have any notion, at this moment, what a National Debt is, or can conceive what a National Store should be, is one of many evil consequences of the lies which, under the title of "Political Economy," have been taught by the ill-educated, and mostly dishonest, commercial men, who at present govern the press of the country.

I have again and again stated the truth in both these matters, but must try once more to do it, emphatically, and intelligibly.

A "civilized nation" in modern Europe consists, in broad terms, of (A) a mass of half-taught, discontented, and mostly penniless populace, calling itself the people; of (B) a thing which it calls a government—meaning an apparatus for collecting and spending money; and (C) a small number of capitalists, many of them rogues, and most of them stupid persons, who have no idea of any object of human existence other than money-making, gambling, or champagne-bibbing. A certain quantity of literary men, saying anything they can get paid to say,—of clergymen, saying anything they have been taught to say,—of natural philosophers, saying anything that comes into their heads,—and of nobility, saying nothing at all, combine in disguising the action, and perfecting the disorganization, of the mass; but with respect to practical business, the civilized nation consists broadly of mob, money-collecting machine, and capitalist.

Now when this civilized mob wants to spend money for any profitless or mischievous purposes,—fireworks, illuminations, battles, driving about from place to place, or what not,—being itself penniless, it sets its money-collecting machine to borrow the sum needful for these amusements from the civilized capitalist.

The civilized capitalist lends the money, on condition that through the money-collecting machine, he may tax the civilized mob thenceforward forever. The civilized mob spends the money forthwith, in gunpowder, infernal machines, masquerade dresses, new boulevards, or anything else it has set its idiotic mind on for the moment; and appoints its money collecting machine to collect a daily tax from its children, and children's children, to be paid to the capitalists from whom it had received the accommodation, thenceforward forever.

That is the nature of a National Debt.

In order to understand that of a National Store, my readers must first consider what any store whatever, serviceable to human beings, consists of. A store properly means a collection of useful things. Literally, it signifies only a quantity, or much of *any*thing. But the heap of broken bottles which, I hear, is accumulating under the principal cliff of Snowdon, through the contributions of tourists from the summit, is not properly to be called a store; though a binfull of old wine is. Neither is a heap of cannon-balls a store;* though a heap of potatoes is. Neither is a cellar full of gunpowder a store; though a cellar full of coals is. A store is, for squirrels, of nuts; for bees, of honey; for men, of food, clothes, fuel, or pretty things, such as toys or jewels,—and, for educated persons, of books and pictures.

And the possession of such a store by the nation would signify, that there were no taxes to pay; that everybody had clothes enough, and some stuff laid by for next year; that everybody had food enough, and plenty of salted pork, pickled walnuts, potted shrimps, or other conserves, in the cupboard; that everybody had jewels enough, and some of the biggest laid by, in treasuries and museums; and, of persons caring for such things, that everybody had as many books and pictures as they could read or look at; with quantities of the highest quality besides, in easily accessible public libraries and galleries.

---

* They may serve for the *defense* of the store, of course;—so may the broken bottles, stuck on the top of a wall. But the lock of your cupboard is not the contents of it.

Now the wretches who have, at present, the teaching of the people in their hands, through the public press, tell them that it is not "practical" to attempt to bring about this state of things;—and that their government, or money-collecting machine, must not buy wine, potatoes, jewels, or pictures for them; but *must* buy iron plates two feet thick, gunpowder and red tape. And this popular instruction is given, you will find, in the end, by persons who know that they could not get a percentage themselves, (without the public's coming to know it,) on buying potatoes or pictures; but *can* get it, and a large one, on manufacturing iron, on committing wholesale murder, or on tying up papers with red tape.

Now the St. George's Company propose to themselves, —and, if the God they believe in, lives, will assuredly succeed in their proposition,—to put an end to this rascally and inhuman state of things, and bring about an honest and human state of them, instead. And they have already actually begun the accumulation of a National Store of good and useful things; by the collection and administration of which, they are not themselves to derive any gain whatsoever, but the Nation only.

We are, therefore, at present, as I said at first, a company established for a charitable purpose; the object of charity being the entire body of the British nation, now paying taxes to cheating capitalists. But we hope to include, finally, in our ranks a large number of the people themselves, and to make quite a different sort of people of them, carrying out our company's laws, to the abolition of many existing interests and in abrogation of many existing arrangements.

And the laws which we hope thus to see accepted are none of them new; but have been already recommended by all wise men, and practiced by all truly prosperous states ; nor is there anything whatever new in the modes of administration proposed ;—and especially be it noted, there is nothing of the present leader's fancies, in any part or character of the scheme—which is merely the application, to our nationally diseased thoughts and practices, of the direct precepts of the true sages of past time, who are every one of them in harmony concerning all that is necessary for men to do, feel, and know.

And we hope to establish these laws, not by violence, but by obeying them ourselves, to the extent of which existing circumstances admit,; and so gradually showing the advantage of them, and making them acceptable to others. Not that, for the enforcement of some of them (the abolition of all manufactures that make the air unwholesome, for instance), we shall hesitate to use the strong hand, when once our hands are strong. But we shall not begin by street riots to throw down our neighbor's chimneys, or break his machinery ;—though what we shall *end* in doing—God knows, not I,—but I have my own thoughts concerning it; not at present needing exposition.

The Companions, for the most part, will remain exactly in the condition of life they held before entering the Society; but they will direct all their powers, and some part of their revenues, in that condition, to the advance of its interests. We hold it shortsighted and ruinous policy to form separate institutions, or attempt the sudden establishment of new systems of labor. Every one of us must use the advantages he now possesses, whatever they may be, and contend with the difficulties arising out of his present position, gradually modifying it, as he can, into conformity with the laws which the Society desires may be ultimately observed by all its members.

The first of our conditions of Companionship is Honesty. We are a company of honest persons, vowing to have no fellowship with dishonest ones. Persons who do not know the meaning of the word "Honesty," or who would in anywise, for selfish convenience, tolerate any manner of cheating or lying, either in others or themselves, we class indiscriminately with the self-conscious rogues, for whom we have more respect; and our separation from all such is to be quite manifest and unmistakable. We do not go into monasteries,—we seek no freedom of conscience in foreign lands,—we profess no severities of asceticism at home. We simply refuse to have any dealings with rogues, whether at home or abroad.

I repeat, for this must be strictly understood; we are a company of honest persons; and will add to ourselves none but persons of that quality. We, for our own part, entirely decline to live by passing bad half-crowns, by selling bad goods, or by lying as to their relative quality. And we hold only such communication with persons guilty of such practices, as we should with any other manner of thieves or liars.

It will follow that anything gravely said by a Companion of St. George may be, without investigation, believed; and anything sold by one, without scrutiny, bought for what it is said to be,—of which recovery of old principles of human speech and commerce, no words can set forth the infinitude of beneficial consequences, when it is once brought about among a discernible and every day increasing body of persons.

The second condition of Companionship is the resolution, so far as we have ability, to earn our own living with our own hands, and not to allow, much less compel, other people to work for us: this duty being of double force,—

first, as necessary to our own health and honor; but much more, as striking home at the ghastly universal crime of modern society,—stealing the laborer's bread from him (making him work, that is to say, for ours, as well as his own), and then abusing and despising him for the degradation of character which his perpetual toil involves;* deliberately, in many cases, refusing to encourage him in economy, that we may have him at our mercy to grind in the mill; always selling as much gin and beer to him as we can persuade him to swill, at the rate of twenty-pence for twopence' worth, (see Letter XXVII.,) to fill our own pockets; and teaching him pious catechisms, that we may keep him our quiet slave.

We cannot, at present, all obey this great law concerning labor, however willing we may be; for we may not, in the condition of life in which we have been brought up, have been taught any manual labor by which we now could make a living. I myself, the present Master of the Society, cannot obey this, its second main law; but then I am only a makeshift Master, taking the place till somebody more fit for it be found. Sir Walter Scott's life, in the full strength of it at Ashestiel, and early at Abbotsford, with his literary work done by ten, or at latest twelve, in the morning; and the rest of the day spent in useful work with Tom Purdie in his woods, is a model of wise moral management of mind and body, for men of true literary power; but I had neither the country training of body, nor have the natural strength of brain, which can reach this ideal in anywise. Sir Walter wrote as a stream flows; but I do all my brain-

---

* See Letter XI. (November, '71,) pages 142 to 145, the most pregnant four pages in the entire series of these letters; and compare that for January of this year, pp. 100—101, and for April, p. 170.

work like a wrung sponge, and am tired out, and good for nothing, after it. Sir Walter was in the open air, farm-bred, and playing with lambs, while I was a poor little Cockney wretch, playing, in a dark London nursery, with a bunch of keys. I do the best I can, and know what ought to be; and that is all the Company really need of me. I would fain, at this moment, both for pleasure and duty's sake, be cutting the dead stems out of my wood, or learning to build a dry stone wall under my good mason, Mr. Usher, than writing these institutes of St. George; but the institutes are needed, and must be written by me, since there is nobody else to write them.

Any one, therefore, may be a Companion of St. George who sincerely does what they can, to make themselves useful, and earn their daily bread by their own labor: and some forms of intellectual or artistic labor, inconsistent (as a musician's) with other manual labor, are accepted by the Society as useful; provided they be truly undertaken for the good and help of all; and that the intellectual laborer ask no more pay than any other workman. A scholar can generally live on less food than a plowman and there is no conceivable reason why he should have more.* And if he be a false-hearted scholar, or a bad painter or fiddler, there is infinite reason why he should have less. My readers may have been surprised at the instant and eager assertion, as of a leading principle, in the first of these letters, (January, '71,) that people cannot live by art. But

---

* Again, I have more myself—but that is because I have been ill-bred; and I shall be most thankful to take less, as soon as other people cease to be paid for doing nothing. People cry out upon me for asking ten shillings for a year's *Fors;* but never object to Mr. Barber's paying his clerk a guinea for opening his study door to me five times, charging the same to St. George's account. (See *Fors* of April, pp. 186, 187, 188).

I spoke swiftly, because the attempt so to live is among the worst possible ways they can take of injurious begging. There are a few, a very few persons born in each generation, whose words are worth hearing; whose art is worth seeing. These born few will preach, or sing, or paint, in spite of you; they will starve like grasshoppers, rather than stop singing; and even if you don't choose to listen, it is charitable to throw them some crumbs to keep them alive. But the people who take to writing or painting as a means of livelihood, because they think it genteel, are just by so much more contemptible than common beggars, in that they are noisy and offensive beggars. I am quite willing to pay for keeping our poor vagabonds in the workhouse; but not to pay them for grinding organs outside my door, defacing the streets with bills and caricatures, tempting young girls to read rubbishy novels, or deceiving the whole nation to its ruin, in a thousand leagues square of dirtily printed falsehood, every morning at breakfast. Whatever in literature, art, or religion, is done for money, is poisonous itself; and doubly deadly, in preventing the hearing or seeing of the noble literature and art which have been done for love and truth. If people cannot make their bread by honest labor, let them at least make no noise about the streets; but hold their tongues, and hold out their idle hands humbly; and they shall be fed kindly.

Then the third condition of Companionship is, that, after we have done as much manual work as will earn our food, we all of us discipline ourselves, our children, and any one else willing to be taught, in all the branches of honorable knowledge and graceful art attainable by us. Having honestly obtained our meat and drink, and having sufficiently eaten and drunken, we proceed, during the rest of the day, to seek after things better than meat, and drink;

and to provide for the nobler necessities of what, in ancient days, Englishmen used to call their souls.

To this end, we shall, as we increase in numbers, establish such churches and schools as may best guide religious feeling, and diffuse the love of sound learning and prudent art. And when I set myself first to the work of forming the Society, I was induced to do so chiefly by the consciousness that the balanced unison of artistic sensibility with scientific faculty, which enabled me at once to love Giotto, and learn from Galileo, gave me singular advantages for a work of this kind. More particularly, the course of study through which, after being trained in the severest schools of Protestant divinity, I became acquainted with the mythology of Greece, and legends of Rome, in their most vivid power over the believing minds of both nations, permits me now to accept with freedom and respect the concurrence of a wider range of persons holding different views on religious subjects, than any other scholar I know, at the present day, in England, would feel himself secure in the hope of reconciling to a common duty, and in uncontested elements of faith.

The scheme, and elementary means, of this common education, I am now occupied in arranging and choosing as I best may.* In especial, I have set myself to write three grammars—of geology, botany, and zoology, which will contain nothing but indisputable facts in those three branches of proper human learning; and which, if I live a little longer, will embrace as many facts as any ordinary schoolboy or schoolgirl need be taught. In these three grammars, (*Deucalion, Proserpina* and *Love's Meinie*,†) I

---

* See *Fors* for January of this year, pp. 109, 110.
† This book I shall extend, if time be given me, from its first proposed form into a parallel one with the two others.

shall accept every aid that sensible and earnest men of science can spare me, toward the task of popular education: and I hope to keep thankful records of the names of the persons who are making true discoveries in any of these sciences, and of the dates of such discovery, which shall be unassailably trustworthy as far as they extend. I hope also to be able to choose, and in some degree provide, a body of popular literature of entirely serviceable quality. Of some of the most precious books needed, I am preparing, with the help of my friends, new editions, for a common possession in all our school libraries.

If I have powers fitted for this task (and I should not have attempted it but in conviction that I have), they are owing mainly to this one condition of my life, that, from my youth up, I have been seeking the fame, and honoring the work, of others;—never my own. I first was driven into literature that I might defend the fame of Turner; since that day I have been explaining the power, or proclaiming the praise, of Tintoret,—of Luini,—of Carpaccio,—of Botticelli,—of Carlyle;—never thinking for an instant of myself: and sacrificing what little faculty, and large pleasure, I had in painting, either from nature or noble art, that, if possible, I might bring others to see what I rejoiced in, and understand what I had deciphered. There has been no heroism in this, nor virtue;—but only, as far as I am myself concerned, quaint ordering of Fate; but the result is, that I *have* at last obtained an instinct of impartial and reverent judgment, which sternly fits me for this final work, to which, if to anything, I was appointed.

And for the right doing of it, and for all future work of the same kind, requiring to be done for the Society by other persons, it is absolutely needful that the person charged with it should be implicitly trusted, and accurately obeyed by the Companions, in all matters necessary to the working of the Society. He cannot lose his time in contention or persuasion; he must act undisturbedly, or his mind will not suffice for its toil; and with concurrence of all the Society's power, or half their power will be wasted, and the whole perverted, by hesitation and opposition. His authority over them must correspond precisely, in the war against the poverty and vice of the State, to that of a Roman Dictator, in his war against its external enemies.

Of a Roman "*Dictator,*" I say, observe: not a Roman "*Emperor.*" It is not the command of private will, but the dictation of necessary law, which the Society obeys:—only, the obedience must be absolute, and without question; faithful to the uttermost,—that is to say, trusting to the uttermost. The practice of faith and obedience to some of our fellow-creatures is the alphabet by which we learn the higher obedience to heaven; and it is not only needful to the prosperity of all noble united action, but essential to the happiness of all noble living spirits.

XI.—THE END OF THE WHOLE MATTER.

THE following series of aphorisms contain the gist of *Fors Clavigera*, and may serve to facilitate the arrangement of its incidental matter.

1. Any form of government will work, provided the governors are real, and the people obey them; and none will work, if the governors are unreal, or the people disobedient. If you mean to have logs for kings, no quantity of liberty in choice of the wood will be of any profit to

you:—nor will the wisest or best governor be able to serve you, if you mean to discuss his orders instead of obeying them. Read carefully on this matter Letter XIII., pp. 176 and 177.

2. The first duty of government is to see that the people have food, fuel, and clothes. The second, that they have means of moral and intellectual education.

3. Food, fuel, and clothes can only be got out of the ground, or sea, by muscular labor; and no man has any business to have any, unless he has done, if able, the muscular work necessary to produce his portion, or to render (as the labor of a surgeon or physician renders), equivalent benefit to life. It indeed saves both toil and time that one man should dig, another bake, and another tan; but the digger, baker, and tanner are alike bound to do their equal day's duty; and the business of the government is to see that they have done it, before it gives any one of them their dinner.

4. While the daily teaching of God's truth, doing of His justice, and heroic bearing of His sword, are to be required of every human soul according to its ability, the mercenary professions of preaching, law-giving, and fighting must be entirely abolished.

5. Scholars, painters, and musicians, may be advisedly kept, on due pittance, to instruct or amuse the laborer after, or at, his work; provided the duty be severely restricted to those who have high special gifts of voice, touch, and imagination;* and that the possessors of these melodious lips, light-fingered hands, and lively brains, do

---

*Such limitation being secured by the severity of the required education in the public schools of art, and thought; and by the high standard of examination fixed, before granting license of exhibition, in the public theaters, or picture galleries.

resolutely undergo the normal discipline necessary to insure their skill; the people whom they are to please, understanding, always, that they cannot employ these tricksy artists without working double-tides themselves, to provide them with beef and ale.

6. The duty of the government, as regards the distribution of its work, is to attend first to the wants of the most necessitous; therefore, to take particular charge of the back streets of every town; leaving the fine ones, more or less, according to their finery, to take care of themselves. And it is the duty of magistrates, and other persons in authority, but especially of all bishops, to know thoroughly the numbers, means of subsistence, and modes of life of the poorest persons in the community, and to be sure that *they* at least are virtuous and comfortable; for if poor persons be not virtuous, after all the wholesome discipline of povery, what must be the state of the rich, under their perilous trials and temptations?*—but, on the other hand, if the poor are made comfortable and good, the rich have a fair chance of entering the kingdom of heaven also, if they choose to live honorably and decently.

7. Since all are to be made to labor for their living, and it is not possible to labor without materials and tools, these must be provided by the government, for all persons, in the

---

* Here is just an instance of what might at first seem to be a jest; but is a serious and straightforward corollary from the eternally true fact stated by St. Timothy: "They that will be rich fall into temptation and a snare, and into many foolish lusts, which drown men in destruction and perdition;" and by Horace:
"Quanto quisque sibi plura negaverit
Ab Dis plura feret."
The passage might at first be thought inconsistent with what is said above of the "degradation" which perpetual toil involves. But toil and poverty are two different things. Poverty ennobles, and secures; toil degrades, and endangers. We are all bound to fulfill our task: but happy only if we can also enter into our rest.

necessary quantities. If bricks are to be made, clay and straw must be provided; if sheep are to be kept, grass; if coats are to be made, cloth; if oakum to be picked, oakum. All these raw materials, with the tools for working them, must be provided by the government, at first, free of cost to the laborer, the value of them being returned to them as the first-fruits of his toil; and no pawnbrokers or usurers may be allowed to live by lending sea to fishermen, air to fowlers, land to farmers, crooks to shepherds, or bellows to smiths.

8. When the lands and seas belonging to any nation are all properly divided, cultivated, and fished, its population cannot be increased, except by importing food in exchange for useless articles,—that is to say, by living as the toy-manufacturers of some independent nation, which can both feed itself, and afford to buy toys besides. But no nation can long exist in this servile state. It must either emigrate, and form colonies to assist in cultivating the land which feeds it, or become entirely slavish and debased. The moment any nation begins to import food,* its political power and moral worth are ended.

9. All the food, clothing, and fuel required by men can be produced by the labor of their own arms on the earth and sea; all food is appointed to be so produced, and *must* be so produced at their peril. If instead of taking the quantity of exercise made necessary to their bodies by God, in the work appointed by God, they take it in hunting or shooting, they become ignorant, irreligious, and

---

* It may always import such food as its climate cannot produce, in exchange for such food as it can; it may buy oranges with corn, or pepper with cheese. But not with articles that do not support life. Separate *cities* may honorably produce saleable art; Limoges its enamel, Sheffield its whittles; but a *nation* must not live on enamel or whittles.

finally insane, and seek to live by fighting as well as by hunting; whence the type of Nimrod in the circle of the Hell-towers, which I desired you to study in Dante. If they do not take exercise at all, they become sensual, and insane in worse ways. *And it is physically impossible that true religious knowledge, or pure morality, should exist among any classes of a nation who do not work with their hands for their bread.* Read Letter XI. carefully.

10. The use of machinery* in agriculture throws a certain number of persons out of wholesome employment, who must thenceforward either do nothing or mischief. The use of machinery in art destroys the national intellect; and, finally, renders all luxury impossible. All machinery needful in ordinary life to supplement human or animal labor may be moved by wind or water; while steam, or any mode of *heat-power*, may only be employed justifiably under extreme or special conditions of need; as for speed on main lines of communication, and for raising water from great depths, or other such work beyond human strength.

11. No true luxury, wealth, or religion is possible to dirty persons; nor is it decent or human to attempt to compass any temporal prosperity whatever by the sacrifice of cleanliness. The speedy abolition of all abolishable filth is the first process of education;† the principles of which I state in the second group of aphorisms following.

---

* Foolish people are continually quibbling and stupefying themselves about the word "machine." Briefly, any instrument is a machine so far as its action is, in any particular, or moment, beyond the control of the human hand. A violin, a pencil, and plow, are tools, not machines. A grinding organ, or a windmill, is a machine, not a tool; often the two are combined; thus a lathe is a machine, and the workman's chisel, used at it, a tool.

† The ghastly squalor of the once lovely fields of Dulwich, trampled into mud, and strewn with rags and paper by the filthy London population, bred in cigar smoke, which is attracted by the Crystal Palace, would alone neutralize all possible gentlemanly education in the district.

12. All education must be moral first; intellectual secondarily. Intellectual, before—(much more without)—moral education, is, in completeness, impossible; and in incompleteness, a calamity.

13. Moral education begins in making the creature to be educated, clean, and obedient. This must be done thoroughly, and at any cost, and with any kind of compulsion rendered necessary by the nature of the animal, be it dog, child, or man.

14. Moral education consists next in making the creature practically serviceable to other creatures, according to the nature and extent of its own capacities; taking care that these be healthily developed in such service. It may be a question how long, and to what extent, boys and girls of fine race may be allowed to run in the paddock before they are broken; but assuredly the sooner they are put to such work as they are able for, the better. Moral education is summed when the creature has been made to do its work with delight, and thoroughly; but this cannot be until some degree of intellectual education has been given also.

15. Intellectual education consists in giving the creature the faculties of admiration, hope, and love.

These are to be taught by the study of beautiful Nature; the sight and history of noble persons; and the setting forth of noble objects of action.

16. Since all noble persons hitherto existent in the world have trusted in the government of it by a supreme Spirit, and in that trust, or faith, have performed all their great actions, the history of these persons will finally mean the history of their faith; and the sum of intellectual education will be the separation of what is inhuman, in such faiths, and therefore perishing, from what is human, and, for human creatures, eternally true.

These sixteen aphorisms contain, as plainly as I can speak it, the substance of what I have hitherto taught, and am now purposed to enforce practice of, as far as I am able. It is no business of mine to think about possibilities;—any day, any moment, may raise up some one to take the carrying forward of the plan out of my hands, or to furnish me with larger means of prosecuting it; meantime, neither hastening nor slackening, I shall go on doing what I can, with the people, few or many, who are ready to help me.

THE END.